JOHN MILTON'S
PARADISE LOST

A SneakerBlossom Paraphrase

by Lisa Pelissier

Thank you to my cover illustrator, who did such gorgeous work:

Annika Pelissier

And to my beta readers:

Jordan Diem
Kailen Fleck

And in memory of and with lasting gratitude to
Ned Brause (1958 – 2025)

TABLE OF CONTENTS

CAVEATS

In its original form, Paradise Lost is a poem in unrhymed iambic pentameter—a meter consisting of ten syllables per line alternating unaccented with accented syllables. I've retained the "unrhymed" part—not too difficult to accomplish—but have not attempted iambic pentameter, largely because if I did, it would first be foolish as I am no poet, but second, it would necessitate word choices and order that would make the text more difficult to understand. I have kept the poetic form in order to give the student some flavor of reading an epic poem. Truly, the "epic" part is the relentless flow of the narrative from beginning to end, something I have retained in retaining the story, I hope.

As with any translation, you miss something when you read a version that was not the author's original. I hope that through these meager efforts, students will come to love the story enough that one day—maybe in a year, maybe in twenty, maybe in fifty—they will dive into this epic poem in its original form.

*Note: This work—even in this abridged and paraphrased form—contains references to historical and mythical characters and places. A list of pertinent references is given at the start of each chapter, and a complete index of those characters and places is provided at the back of the book to aid in comprehension. Characters who play a role in the story itself are not included. References are only listed for the chapter in which they first appear.

*Note 2: I did not attempt to convert suppress Milton's opinions in order to modernize them. As such, you may notice references that would be considered unseemly, such as his musings about women.

INTRODUCTION

William Faithorne, Public domain,
via Wikimedia Commons

John Milton was born to a Protestant family in London, England, in 1606. His father was a scrivener, someone who wrote things for people who could not read and write—the majority of the English at that time.

John was a good student and entered the University of Cambridge when he was fifteen. After college, he returned home to care for his parents until his mother's death (1637), at which time he went abroad to increase his education and meet with other educated people, beginning in France and Italy. Hearing that England was on the cusp of civil war, he returned home, where he spent his time studying the classics, learning scholarly and current languages, writing, and tutoring his nephews. He married 17-year-old Mary Powell at age 34. After ten years and four children, his wife died. He remarried in 1656 and again being widowed, married a third wife in 1663.

He wrote much about freedom of speech and freedom of the press. He was against the concept of monarchy and wanted a free republican form of government for his country, particularly during the English Civil War (1642-1651) when King Charles was overthrown. His works were very influential in convincing people that government should be by consent of the people governed, and his writings—and those of others—influenced the American colonists to revolution. He served as a member of the English republican government from 1649 to 1660. When the monarchy was restored in 1660, he went into hiding for a time.

By 1652, Milton was completely blind. *Paradise Lost* was written entirely after he lost his sight, dictated to aides who wrote it down for him. It was immediately recognized as a great epic, with many asserting that Milton was second only to Shakespeare as the greatest English writer.

His influence on the world of literature was enormous, from his use of unrhymed verse and syncopated meter to his descriptive language and moral sense. His devotion to personal freedom and attention to his own moral compass came through in his innovations in writing. For centuries, writers have emulated his style and themes, including, among others, Mary Shelley, in her most famous work, *Frankenstein*.

BOOK I REFERENCES

Adonis *(god):* In ancient Greek mythology, Adonis is the epitome of masculine beauty and the lover of several goddesses, especially Aphrodite

Baalam *(man):* Biblical prophet who refused to curse Israel (see Numbers 22-24); Also known for encouraging the Israelites to defile themselves with Midianite women (Numbers 31:16)

Camelot *(place):* The mythical British kingdom of King Arthur

Charlemagne *(man):* King of the Franks and Lombards; Later the first Holy Roman Emperor (lived 747-814 AD)

cherub (cherubim is plural) *(angel/s):* Winged angelic beings who guarded the Tree of Life after the fall of man; See Ezekiel 10:9-17 for a description

Isis *(goddess):* Egyptian goddess later worshipped by the ancient Greeks and Romans

Israel *(people):* The people of God in the Old Testament of the Bible

Leviathan *(animal):* Enormous sea beast spoken of in Job 41 and Psalm 74:14, often identified as a sea serpent, dragon, or (later) a crocodile or whale

Moloch *(god):* Canaanite god who was known for enjoying child sacrifices

Muse(s) *(goddess(es)):* Greek goddesses of the arts, said to inspire poetry, music, and stories

Osiris *(god):* Egyptian god of death and rebirth

Troy *(place):* Site of the Trojan War, the subject of Homer's *Iliad*

Venus *(goddess):* Roman goddess of love and sexuality

BOOK 1

Milton:

Sing, oh heavenly Muse,
Of how Earth and Heaven began,
Arising from nothing.

Sing of Adam's loss
When he ate the fruit in the garden
And brought mankind to destruction.

Sing of the One who will bring restoration.

And help me as I tell this tale.
Help me rise above my sinful heart.
Help me brighten my darkness
So that I can defend God before men.

Narrator:

Adam and Eve, who were loved by God,
Chose to disobey His will.
They were tempted by the serpent, Satan,
Who fought against God and Heaven,
And tried to seize glory for himself.

God hurled the devil and his legions
Into the fiery, bottomless pit.
There they will dwell in chains and fire,
Dead, even though they cannot die.

Satan is filled with anger and hate
At the sight of the fiery furnace,
Seeing the flames that cast darkness instead of light.
He is far from God in the home justice made for him.

Satan turns to his companion, Beelzebub, and speaks.

Satan:

Beelzebub? Is it really you I see looking so grim?
Our fight has ended in ruin.
Who knew God was so strong?
But I'm not sorry.
I am still myself.
I still have me.
And I still desire to stand against God.
I'm not going to bow to Him or beg for mercy.
Maybe we can't win the war,
But we can fight for all eternity.

Beelzebub:

Oh Prince and my leader,
You led us in war and endangered the throne of God.
Was He really that strong,
Or was it just chance that caused us to lose?
We have lost our glory.
We are swallowed up in misery.
But we still have our minds and spirits.
Maybe we can become strong again,
But if we do, God will make us His slaves,
Doing His work here in the fires of Hell.
What is the use in trying to become stronger?

Satan:

We will always adore doing evil
Because it is the thing God does not want.

If God tries to use us for His good and noble purposes,
We need to turn his good to evil.
Look! The firestorm has stopped, and all is quiet.
Let's gather all the demons together
And discuss how we can offend God
And make things better for ourselves.

Narrator:

Then Satan stretched his body across the burning lake.
He was as big as the giants of legend,
Like Leviathan, a sea beast so large
That sailors mistook him for an island
And tried to anchor their ships in his scaly flesh.

He lay there, plotting his evil deeds,
And bringing further damnation on his head.
He never understood the infinite grace and mercy
That would result from his malicious seduction
Or the wrath that would come on his own head.

Satan strains against the chains that bind him.
He breaks free and rises in clouds of billowing smoke.
Stretching his wings, he flies to the shore
And lands amid the noxious stench of sulfur.
Beelzebub joins him
And they both admire their own strength
And survey the landscape.

Satan:

So this is the dark and gloomy land
For which we traded the light of Heaven.
Say goodbye to joy and happiness,
And hello to the horrors of deepest Hell.
It doesn't matter where I am.
Heaven and Hell are only states of mind.
I am still free.

God won't kick us out of Hell,
So here we can reign without worry.
Better to reign in Hell than serve in Heaven.
Call the others so we can begin to reclaim Heaven,
Or at least drag it down to Hell with us.

Beelzebub:

No one but God Himself could have conquered you.
Let the others take heart.
We will rise from this fiery grave at your command.

Narrator:

Satan moved toward the shore.
His shield was as large as the Moon.
His spear was as big as the tallest pine.
Every step he took scorched his feet with fire
But he put up with it until he came to the shore of the flaming sea.
He called to the fallen angels
Whose bodies choked the burning streams of Hell.

Satan:

My warriors! My princes! Eternal spirits!
Are you lying in the fire napping?
From your posture it looks like you've given up,
Like you're bowing to your Conqueror.
He's coming to trample us down.
He will strike us with bolts of lightning.
Awake! Arise before it is too late!

Narrator:

The demons heard him and leapt up.
They were ashamed of themselves,
But they didn't yet understand what had happened.
They hadn't felt the pain of the fire yet.

They rose like a plague of locusts, filling the sky.
At Satan's command, they landed on the plain.
They were god-like, more than human.
For in the future, they would corrupt the heart of man.
They would turn man to worship animals instead of God.
Mankind will worship devils as gods
And make temples for them in the temples of God.
These demons can take the form of humans,
For a spirit being is not bound by flesh.
They receive the bloody human sacrifices given to Moloch.
They masquerade as Isis and Osiris, Venus and Adonis.
They would lead Israel to worship Baalam
And to make a golden calf to be a god.
They would corrupt priests,
Bringing lust and violence to the house of God.

All these flocked to Satan's court.
They were damned but not despairing.
Courage and hope filled them
As they saw Satan standing proud and firm,
Ready to do battle once again.

Azaziel, a tall cherub, stood at Satan's right.
He held the golden banner of Hell.
Trumpets called for war.
Ten thousand banners rose in the air.
A forest of spears, too vast to measure,
Rose in perfect formation.
They breathed together as one,
Unafraid and cold-blooded.
Their blistering feet stood on the ground of Hell,
As they awaited the command of their chief.

Satan's eyes roved over the troops,
Measuring his army, as glorious as gods.
His heart swelled with pride.
Such an army has never been seen in human history,
Not at Troy or Camelot, with Charlemagne, or among the Turks.

Satan stood above them like a tower.
He shone brightly, but not as bright as he had been.
Proud and glorious he stood, intent on revenge.
The spirits around him, too, were less than they had been,
They had been flung from Heaven.
Their glory had withered.
He tried to speak but failed and wept instead.
Three times he tried and failed,
And at last, his words found their way.

Satan:

Oh immortal spirits! Oh powers unparalleled!
The change that has come upon us is dire.
But we can rise to Heaven once more.
We underestimated God's strength.
Now that we know his power, our strategy must change.
He has conquered us by force.
Now we must win by our wits.
God is planning to create new worlds.
We must destroy them.
We will never be at peace, but we can't give up.
We must fight, whether openly or in secret.

Narrator:

The demons raged against God.
Their uplifted swords reflected the light of hellfire.
They beat their swords on their shields in a warlike tune,
Defying God in His Heaven.

In the distance was a mountain,
Belching sulfurous smoke and fire.
Mammon, the lowest of the demons,
Led a number of them toward the mountain
Armed with spades and pickaxes,
Ready to mine the mineral wealth within it.
Even before the fall, Mammon loved wealth.

He loved Heaven's golden streets more than he loved God.
It was Mammon who would teach men
To ransack the Earth for its treasures.
Mammon and his brigade soon opened a gash in the mountain
And dug out ribs of gold, glowing with reflected hellfire.
From these riches, the demons quickly built a golden temple.
They filled it with magical hanging lamps, full of starlight and fire.
No greater temple has been seen in all human history.

The trumpets called a council to be held.
Pandemonium, they called their new capital.
The demons swarmed thickly in the air and in the ground,
Flying to and fro like bees.
They made themselves small so they would fit
In the hall of Satan's infernal court.
After a short silence, the meeting began.

BOOK 2 REFERENCES

Acheron *(place):* The river of pain in the underworld of ancient Greek mythology

Cocytus *(place):* The river of wailing in the underworld of ancient Greek mythology

Lethe *(place):* The river of forgetfulness in the underworld of Ancient Greek mythology

Medusa *(woman):* In Greek mythology, Medusa is a woman who was cursed to have living snakes as hair. A single glance at her hideousness was enough to turn a person to stone.

Phlegethon *(place):* The river of fire in the underworld of ancient Greek mythology

Styx *(place):* The river of hate in the underworld of the ancient Greeks.

BOOK 2

The demons plan their attack.
Satan joins with his offspring, Sin and Death, to begin it.

Narrator:

Satan sat on a rich and sumptuous throne,
Glorying in his evil hopes of war against Heaven.

Satan:

Heaven can be taken.
No one can hold us back.
We are immortal, but even more importantly,
If we rise again after such a great fall,
Our glory will be that much greater.
We will never be beaten again.
We have a kind of unity Heaven can never have.

In Heaven, one may envy another's greatness.
Here, to envy is to long for greater pain,
For that is all we have.
Who could covet more of what has been given to us?
Therefore, there can be no envy among us,
No disharmony like that.
We are more sure of victory now
Than we were when we first fought.
All we have to do is decide:
Will it be by war or by trickery that we shall attain the victory?

Narrator:

Moloch, the fiercest and strongest of them, rose.
He believed himself to be equal to God,
And would rather be nothing than be less than that.
He despised his own life.
He had no fear of God or Hell or anything else.

Moloch:

I say we go to war.
Leave trickery to the cunning.
We have an army ready to fight.
Delaying will only give more power to God
And more suffering to us.
Let's bring the sulfurous fires of Hell to Heaven.
He created this blazing misery.
Let it overtake His throne.
Maybe you think this is too difficult.
But don't forget that Heaven is our rightful place.
It's Hell that's unnatural to us.
The journey to Hell was an exhausting climb.
Going to Heaven, our home, will be downhill all the way.
Are you afraid of what God will do to you?
What worse could He do than this?
The only thing that would be worse would be annihilation.
And think about it.
That's not truly worse.
So we have no reason to fear.
We'll either become nothing
Or we'll come right back here.
Even if we don't win, at least we'll have revenge.

Narrator:

Moloch frowned in disapproval at those who looked afraid.
Then the graceful and slick Belial arose.
His voice was pleasant and persuasive,
Despite his evil and corrupt heart.

Belial:

I would be in favor of open war, my friends,
But the very reasons Moloch offers in favor of war
Are, in fact, reasons to oppose it.
We are strong, but the best we can hope for is revenge.
Heaven will be expecting us to attack.
They will post guards in the towers of Heaven.
They will send scouts to watch for us.
If we come with darkness, Heaven's light will cast it out.
All we will achieve is the wrath of God.
Maybe we can make Him angry enough to destroy us,
But who knows if that's even possible?
We go to war hoping for annihilation,
But do you think we can make God do our will?
What if he doesn't destroy us?
What if He makes the fires of Hell hotter?
What if He thinks of something worse?
Maybe we'll be swept into feverish whirlwinds,
Or sunk in a boiling ocean,
Or wrapped in chains, groaning forever!
Then, we would be worse off than we are now.
I am against war.
Maybe if we wait, God's wrath will dim.
Maybe the fires of Hell will die down
And our darkness will turn to light.
This is our only hope—not to earn more Hell.

Narrator:

Belial, therefore, counseled them to laziness and ease.
After this, Mammon spoke.

Mammon:

We are fighting either to dethrone God
Or to restore our place in Heaven.
I say they are both the same thing.

If we return to Heaven without dethroning God
We will have to obey his odious laws.
We will have to delight in being his slaves.
How wearisome!
Why should we worship One we hate?
I'd rather have liberty than slavery and bootlicking.
We ought to be our own masters.
We can thrive here in the darkness.
We used to be the light of Heaven.
We can be the light here too.
Hell is full of gems and gold.
We can make this our magnificent home.
Our torments will become our strength.
We will become the torment itself.
Put aside these thoughts of war.

Narrator:

Hell was filled with wondrous applause.
No one wanted a fate worse than Hell.
They were afraid of the sword of Michael,
Which had conquered them before.
The idea of a Hellish empire delighted them.
It would be the opposite of Heaven,
But just as strong.

Then Beelzebub rose, severe and stately.
His majesty shone strong against the ruin of what he had been.
The demons couldn't help but stare.

Beelzebub:

Why should we renounce our heavenly titles
And embrace the name of Princes of Hell?
God made this to be our prison,
Not our refuge and our safe space.
He is still ruling all of you.
Why are we discussing whether to make war?

The war is over. We lost.
But there is another way to get revenge.
If the prophecies are true, God is about to create a world
And fill it with a race of beings called "men."
They will be like us, great and powerful,
But God will love them more than He loved us.
We must study these creatures.
We must learn their strengths and weaknesses.
Heaven is well defended,
But this new world may be vulnerable.
Maybe there we can find our victory.
We can either destroy the new world with the fires of Hell
Or we can win its inhabitants to our side.
Then, together with them, we can war against God.
God would no longer rejoice in our misfortune,
But only grieve for our victory.
This is the better way.
Why sit around planning a useless hellish empire?

Narrator:

Beelzebub said it, but the thoughts were Satan's.
Who else could have thought of such a devilish plan?
So the demons voted, and Beelzebub spoke again.

Beelzebub:

The vote is concluded and concluded well.
We shall be lifted out of this misery eventually.
But whom shall we send to find this new world?
Who is strong enough to break free from this bottomless abyss?
Who can get past the angels guarding the edges of Hell?
We must choose carefully.
All our hopes rest on him.

Narrator:

Beelzebub stopped here, waiting for a volunteer.
But all the demons were silent.
No one wanted to take the risk.
At last Satan, conscious of his position as king, spoke.

Satan:

You are wise to be cautious.
The way out of Hell is long and hard.
Our prison is strong and surrounded by fire.
Even if someone gets past the gates,
He will only enter nothingness.
And after that, who knows?
But if fear can stop me from trying then I wouldn't be a worthy king.
If I am to have the honor, I ought to have the danger too.
Stay here, mighty ones.
Do whatever eases your suffering.
I will travel to find deliverance for us.
I will go alone.

Narrator:

Satan stopped there and would not let anyone respond.
He was smart to forbid a response.
If anyone went with him, then part of the glory would be theirs.
The demons bowed and worshipped Satan,
Praising him for sacrificing his safety for theirs.

The council was dissolved, and the demons marched away.
Trumpeters proclaimed the decision of the court.
Each demon wandered away to amuse himself
While he waited for the return of his chief.
Some of the demons played at battle.
Others became like angry volcanoes, shooting rocks into the air.
Still others, quieter ones, sang songs to their own glory.
Some sat on hills pondering philosophy:

What is providence? What is fate?
What does it mean to be free?
What is good? What is evil?
What is honorable and what is not?
It didn't do them any good, but it made them feel better.
Other demons went adventuring though Hell,
Trying to find a region that was less painful.

Hell has four rivers that empty into the burning lake.
Styx is the flood of hate.
Acheron is the river of sorrow.
The waters of Cocytus are full of wailing.
And Phlegethon's rolling fires are full of rage.
Another river, Lethe, brings blessed forgetfulness.
But no one can drink of the Lethe.
Medusa guards the way, and the waters remain out of reach.
Beyond Lethe is a frozen land,
So cold it burns like fire.
The adventuring demons find no rest,
Only fire, ice, death, and monsters so horrible
That even fairy tales could not have invented them.

Satan flew on his horrible wings up to the gates of Hell.
There are nine unbreakable gates,
Three of brass, three of iron, and three of diamond.
A guard stands on either side of the gates.
One guard has the body of a woman but the tail of a snake.
The hounds of Hell bark hideously around her.
The other form is more shadow than shape, black as night.
It wears a crown where its head might be.
Satan drew near.
The terrible monster arose.

Satan:

Where are you from? What are you?
Why do you stand in my way?
I'm going through the gates with or without your permission.

Retreat or beware.
You'll learn not to argue with an immortal spirit of Heaven.

Monster:

Are you the one who first rebelled against Heaven?
The one who took a third of the angels with him?
Aren't you one of those condemned to an eternity of pain?
Why do you call yourself a spirit of Heaven?
I am king here.
Go back to your punishment quickly
Or I will whip you with a whip of scorpions.

Narrator:

As the grisly monster spoke, he grew ten times his size.
He was more deformed and hideous than before.
Satan was not afraid.
They gazed at each other, full of hatred.
They were well matched.
Who knows what would have happened
If the snaky sorceress had not intervened?

The Woman:

Why do you lift your hand against your father?
Or you against your son?
If you destroy each other, you will be doing the will of God.

Satan:

What are you saying?
Who are you?
Why would you say that this monster is my son?
I don't know you, and I don't know him.
I've never seen anything as horrible as the two of you.

The Woman:

Have you forgotten me, then?
Once you thought I was beautiful.
Am I so changed?
Don't you remember what happened in Heaven?
While you were rebelling, a sudden pain seized you.
You were blinded by a burst of flame.
The left side of your head split open, and I came out,
A goddess fully armed.
All Heaven was amazed.
They flinched and called me "Sin"
And foretold of evils that would happen because of me.
But many were pleased by me.

You fell in love with me and took me as your own.
I conceived your child.
When you fell from Heaven, I fell too.
I was given the key so I could keep the gates of Hell shut.
So I sat here, thoughtful and waiting for my child to be born.
At last, this monster was born—your own son.
He tore his way out of my body.
He is the destroyer.
He is Death.
He pursued me and ravaged me.
When he had done his worst, I gave birth to his children,
The monsters that now surround me.
Now all of them return to me to beget more of their kind.
I never rest.
And my son, Death, watches them and eggs them on.
He would like to destroy me,
But he knows that doing so would destroy him too.

Stay away from him, Father.
You may have been born in Heaven,
But only God is immortal.

Satan:

My dear daughter,
And my son, born of that sweet but sad affair.
I am not your enemy.
I have come to set you free.
I seek a place where a new race of creatures will be born.
I must find them.
Then I can bring you and Death to a place of happiness,
A place where you can eat your fill,
And all that lives shall be your prey.

Narrator:

Satan stopped speaking, for Sin and Death were pleased.
Death grinned a ghastly smile.
Sin, Death's mother, rejoiced.

The Woman, Sin:

By God's command, I hold the key to the gate.
But why should I feel any loyalty toward God?
He is the One who confined me to the agonies of Hell.
You, my father, gave me myself.
You will bring me to a new world of light and comfort.
I will reign there beside you, your daughter and your darling.

Narrator:

The woman Sin took the key and put it in the lock.
Every bolt and bar unfastened,
And with a jarring sound, the gates opened.
The thunder of it shook all Hell.

They could now see the secrets outside the gate.
A limitless ocean, without measure or time,
Where night and chaos dwell in anarchy and confusion.
There is no order here.

The seeds of the four elements battle for mastery:
Hot, cold, moist, and dry.
First one prevails and then another, for they are ruled by chaos.

Satan stared into the wild abyss.
Was it the womb of nature?
Was it nature's grave?
It wasn't water or land or air or fire
But it was like bits of these all combined,
Waiting for God to command them to become new worlds.

Satan pondered the journey he was to take.
Finally, he spread his wings
And ascended into nothingness.
His wings beat in vain.
Errant winds of fire and sulfur tossed him through the air.
He couldn't walk or fly or swim,
But his motions were like all of these.
A violent noise assaulted him, and he crawled toward it.

Satan came to the throne of blackest Night.
Night was surrounded by his courtiers:
Rumor, Chance, Tumult, Confusion, Discord, and others.

Satan:

Oh you powers of the abyss!
I don't want to pry into your secrets.
I'm only passing through.
Please tell me where the boundary between chaos and Heaven lies.
Or, if our mutual enemy has recently conquered some of your land,
Tell me how to go there.
That is the place I seek.
I will return that land to its original darkness.
This will be good for you and good for me.

Night:

I know who you are, stranger.
You tried to overthrow God.
I saw you being pursued into the deep.
My realm is dwindling.
First Hell was created from it, wide and deep.
Now the universe has been hung from Heaven with a golden chain.
If you're looking for the universe, you don't have far to go.
Go quickly and destroy whatever you can.

Narrator:

Satan did not stay to answer Night.
Encouraged, he sprang upward,
Fighting his way through the elements.

Something strange happened then.
Sin and Death followed him.
They made a trail through the abyss.
It was a trail of wondrous light,
Bridging the gap between Hell and the frail Earth.
The perverse spirits can now travel easily,
Coming to tempt and punish mortals,
Unless God prevents it.

At last, the heavenly light strikes away the darkness.
Order triumphs over chaos.
Satan's path becomes easier when he can see his destination.
In the distance he sees Heaven, wide and rich.
Hanging from a golden chain, he sees the universe of order,
Newly created and doomed, nonetheless.
Full of revenge and cursing, Satan rushes toward it.

BOOK 3 REFERENCES

aether *(reference):* According to ancient and medieval cosmology, as well as pre-19th century scientists, aether was the fifth element, after earth, fire, air, and water. The aether was the substance through which light waves traveled and was present in space outside of the Earth's atmosphere. There is still uncertainty about the existence of aether.

Babel *(place):* In the Bible, Babel is the site of a tower built to reach to the heavens. God confused the languages of those building it, so they weren't able to complete the tower.

Elysian fields *(place):* Part of the ancient Greek underworld, the Elysian fields were akin to paradise, where the good and brave souls went after death.

Empedocles *(man):* Philosopher who theorized that all matter was made of four elements: earth, water, air, and fire

Limbo *(place):* In Roman Catholic doctrine, Limbo is the border between Heaven and Hell, a holding place for the dead prior to the resurrection of Christ and their salvation and for unbaptized believers.

Maeonides *(man):* Homer, author of the *Iliad* and the *Odyssey*

Mount Niphates *(place):* The place Satan lands on Earth

Mount Zion *(place):* While Mount Zion can refer to a particular hill in Jerusalem, it's also a symbol of God's kingdom, the hill from which He rules.

Phineas *(man):* Blind king from ancient Greek mythology who was also a seer

Thamyris *(man):* Ancient Greek singer condemned to blindness after he challenged the Muses to a musical contest and lost

Tiresias *(man):* Blind prophet from ancient Greek literature

Zion *(place):* The holy land of God, sometimes referring to a specific hill in Jerusalem, sometimes to Jerusalem itself, and sometimes to a more spiritual land of God

BOOK 3

God, knowing what will happen, creates His plan of salvation.
Satan stops at the Moon to ask for directions.

Milton:

Oh for a glimpse of the light.
You, Satan, had the light of God in you.
You existed before the Sun and the Heavens.
I see you now, escaped from the fiery lake of Hell.
While I was singing of chaos and eternal night,
My eyes looked for your piercing brightness,
But I couldn't find you.
I'm a blind man, after all.
Yet I walk with the Muses.
Their holy music enchants me.

But I prefer Zion, the holy land of God.
I visit it every night and remember those who were blind like me:
Thamyris, Maeonides, Tiresias, Phineas.
I am like a bird singing in the night.
There is no evening or morning for me.
I can't see the spring flowers
Or the face of God reflected in the faces of my fellow men.
No more knowledge can enter my mind
Through the door of my eyes.
So shine inward, celestial light.
Illuminate my mind and make me see clearly there
So I can describe the things no mortal eye can see.

Narrator:

God the Father looked down from Heaven
To see the works He had created.

At His right sat his only Son.
The shining image of His glory.
On Earth He saw our first parents,
The only two humans yet to exist,
Living in their happy garden of love and joy.
He saw Hell and the space between Heaven and Hell.
He saw Satan, weary and drifting,
Trying to decide where to land.

God the Father:

My Son, see the rage that drives our enemy?
No chains of Hell could hold him back.
He is bent in his desperate revenge.
But it will backfire and return on his own rebellious head.
He is flying toward this newly created world,
Aiming to destroy mankind by force
Or corrupt him by trickery.
He will corrupt him.
Man will listen to the lies oozing out of him.
He will easily disobey the one command I have given him.
He will fall, and all his descendants will fall with him.
It will be his own fault.
I gave him everything he needed to be able to stand.

But like all the ethereal powers,
Man is free to stand or free to fall.
If they weren't free, how could they prove their loyalty?
Or their faith?
Or their love?
If I planned everything for them,
If they had no choice,
Then how could such obedience please Me?
If they didn't have freedom, then what use are will and reason?
Man would be a slave to necessity,
Instead of a servant of God.
They have no excuse.
They cannot blame their Maker or their making.

They themselves engineered their own revolt.
Even though I can foresee their rebellion
I did not cause it.
I will not change their nature.
I made them free.
They will make themselves fall.
But since their fall happens because of Satan's deceit,
Mankind shall find grace.
Satan and the spirits with him shall find none.
Mercy and justice shall both increase my glory,
But mercy will shine more brightly.

Narrator:

At God's word all the angels were filled with joy.
The Son of God was the image of the Father,
Full of endless love and grace without measure.

God the Son:

How full of grace You are, My Father!
Heaven and Earth will praise You
With songs that swirl around your throne.
Extending Your grace to mankind is the right thing to do.
If You withheld grace, Your enemy would win.
Evil would win and Your goodness would lose.
Satan would still be condemned to Hell,
But he would drag all mankind there with him.
The only other thing You could have done
Was to unmake all of Your glorious creation.

God the Father:

Oh my Son, in Whom I delight,
You have spoken my thoughts out loud.
Not all mankind shall be lost.
I will save by My will and grace.
He is weak because he surrenders his strength to sin.

But I will lift him up.
Once again, he will stand against the enemy.
He will know his own weakness.
He will know that I alone have saved him.
I have chosen some specific men.
The others will hear my call and my warning.
I will clear their dark minds and soften their stony hearts.
They will pray
And repent
And obey.
I will see them.
I will hear them.
I will give them a guide called conscience.
If they listen to it, they will find grace and salvation.
Those who neglect My call will be hardened all the more.
They shall become more blind.
They shall stumble into a deeper fall.
Man disobeys and breaks his bond with Heaven.
There is no way for him to undo this treason.
He and his descendants must die.
If they don't, then justice is dead.
The only way for man to live
Is for someone else to die for him,
To pay his debt willingly.
Where shall we find such love?
Which of you, spirits, will become mortal
To redeem man from his fatal crime?
Is there any in Heaven with such great love?

Narrator:

He asked, but the angels were silent.
No one was found to intercede for man,
Much less to die for him.
If it weren't for the Son of God,
The One who is full of love,
All mankind would have been lost.

God the Son:

Father, may it be as You have said.
Man shall find grace.
They do not look for it.
They cannot look for it.
They are dead in their sins and lost.
I will be the redeemer.
Life for life.
Death for death.
Me for him.
Let your anger fall on Me.
I will become a man.
I will leave your side,
Leave your glory,
And die.
Let death rage against Me.
It cannot do so for long.
You have given Me eternal life.
Even though I will submit to Death,
You will not leave me in the grave.
I will rise, victorious,
And deprive My enemy of his prey.
I will give Death a mortal wound.
I will take away his power.
You will look down from Heaven and smile.
I will ruin all my foes, even Death.
Then I and My redeemed shall enter Heaven.
We shall see Your face, my Father.
We shall see peace in it instead of anger.

God the Father:

You are the only peace to be found for man.
You are my comfort.
You know I love all my creations.
For the sake of man, I will lose You for a time.
You will become a Man among men on Earth,

Made flesh and born of a virgin.
Adam's son, yet Adam's lord.
As in Adam all perish,
So in You all shall be saved.
In Adam's sin all were lost.
Only those who repent and live in You will receive life.
You will not lose your own nature.
You are God's Son by birthright
And by Your own merit,
For You are God.
You have more love than You have glory.
By becoming man, you do not lower Yourself,
But raise the state of being human.
From then on You will sit on Your throne
Wearing human flesh.
You shall be both God and Man,
The anointed, universal King.
Every knee shall bow in Heaven, on Earth, and in Hell.
You shall judge the living and the dead,
Men and angels.
Hell will fill up and be secured forever.
Then the world shall burn
And from the ashes a new universe shall arise.
It will be a place of love, joy, truth, and goodness.
You will live with them there.
Adore the Son and give Him honor,
For He shall die to bring this about.

Narrator:

The angels gave a joyful shout.
Heaven rang with their cries of hosanna.
They bowed toward the throne
And cast their golden crowns onto the glittering pavement.
Then they began to sing.

Angels:

You, Our Father, Eternal King!
Omnipotent, Immutable, Immortal!
Infinite King, Author of all being!
Fountain of light, yet in light invisible!
You, Oh Son, are the first-born of all creation.
You are the image of the Father!

All of God's glory and power rests in You!
You will repay Heaven's foes and bring vengeance.
You pity man and have offered to die for his sin.
Oh love that can never be equaled!
Hail Son of God and Savior of Men!
Whenever I praise the Father, I will praise You!

Narrator:

They sang for many happy hours.
Meanwhile, Satan strode back and forth,
Trying to find his prey.
But none could be found.

I can see what will happen in the future.
Once sin has filled the works of men with uselessness and pride,
Men will fix their hopes on fame and pleasure.
Their works are empty and cannot rise above the Earth.
They don't even rise to the level of the Moon.

Spirits higher than men but lower than angels live on the Moon.
These are the giants who came into the ancient world,
Fathering children with human mothers.
These built Babel hoping for glory.
Consider Empedocles, who bragging he was a god,
Threw himself into the volcano at Mount Etna.
Or those who come with robes and hoods, relics and beads,

Indulgences, dispenses, pardons, and bulls flying in the wind.[1]
They will arrive only in Limbo, the paradise of fools.

But now, in the beginning, the Earth is empty.
All over the cosmos Satan wandered
Until he saw the light of dawn in the distance.
He ascended the hill to the wall of Heaven,
A rich structure covered with diamond and gold
With gems glittering in the light of the rising Sun.
Stairs led to the gate,
And underneath the stairs flowed a sea of liquid pearl.
The stairs were let down,
Either to dare Satan to try to climb
Or to taunt him with his sad exclusion from Heaven.
A passage opened over Mount Zion, the promised land
So that God's angels could visit His people often.

Satan looked down on the Earth with wonder,
So far beneath him.
Without hesitation Satan plunged down in flight,
Through the Stars,
Past other worlds,
And entered the air.

Satan alit on the Sun,
A place brighter than words can say.
It is not earth or metal or stone,
But is like all of them, glowing with fire.
Here, rivers run with gold as pure as water,
And the Sun mixes the elements to produce many precious things.

Satan was not impressed.
The light was so bright that nothing cast a shadow.
In the light, Satan could see far.
He saw the angel of the Sun, the one that John saw[2].
The angel was concentrating, lost in thought.
His golden hair mingled with his glorious wings.
Satan saw a helper here,

Someone who could guide him on his grim journey.
But first he must change his shape.
He became a cherub, youthful and innocent,
With wings of rainbow and gold.
The angel of the Sun turned toward him.
It was Urial, one of the seven sentinels of God.

Satan:

Uriel! Great spirit of Heaven!
Most honored son of God!
I have an overwhelming desire to see the wondrous works of God,
Specifically man, for whom God made these things.
Tell me, on which of these shining globes does man live?
Or does he move between them?
I wish to see the one whom God created
To replace the rebellious fiends He drove into Hell.

Narrator:

Uriel did not understand.
Neither angels nor men can discern hypocrisy.
That is an invisible evil that only God can see.
The innocent are not suspicious.
The good do not expect wrongdoing.
Uriel was deceived by Satan's ruse.

Uriel:

Fair angel, your desire is honorable!
The works of God are wonderful and many.
I saw how God made the world out of chaos and confusion.
The elements became obedient to His command.
Then darkness fled, and light and order came.
Earth, water, air, fire, and Heaven's aether combined
And rolled into spheres and turned into Stars.
See below us?
It is the Earth, the home of men.

The light is called "day."
In the darkness, the Moon shines with reflected glory
To lighten the Earth.
See below us?
This is Paradise, the home of Adam.
I cannot take you there, but you will find it easily.

Narrator:

Uriel turned, and Satan bowed to him.
Then Satan sped toward the Earth,
Not stopping until he landed on Mount Niphates.

Book 3 Endnotes

(1) Those who come with robes, hoods, relics, and beads refers to the Roman
    Catholic Church. During the Protestant Reformation just prior to John
    Milton's time, part of the protest was about indulgences (pardons for sin that
    could be bought with money), and decrees from the church that were made
    according to personal whim and/or not according to the principles in the
    Bible.
(2) The apostle John saw a vision of an angel in the book of Revelation.

BOOK 4 REFERENCES

Eden *(place):* The original home of Adam and Eve in the Bible, a garden of paradise

BOOK 4

Satan gets his first glimpse of mankind.
The angelic army begins their strategic defense.

Narrator:

Oh for a voice of warning!
Oh for a voice to help them escape the deadly plans of their enemy!
Satan is bold but not quick.
He is ready to attempt his attack,
But he recoils,
Distracted by horror and doubt,
Which stir up the Hell inside him.
He has fled from Hell
But he is never far from it.
Hell lives inside him.
Satan remembers what he was like before
And the bitterness overwhelms him.
He knows that if he does more evil
He will receive more punishment.
He gazes toward Eden, toward Heaven,
And toward the blazing Sun.

Satan:

I hate the light of the Sun.
I used to be bright like that.
I was glorious until pride and ambition threw me down.
God didn't deserve to be treated like that.
He created me bright and did me no wrong.
I owed Him praise and thanks.
But He made me too good, too lofty.
I was so high that I hated not to be the highest.

I abandoned the debt I owed Him.
I forgot how much I still needed Him.
I didn't understand that gratitude is not a burden.
I would have been happy if He had made me more inferior.
I wouldn't have hoped for more.
I mean, unless another angel wanted to become great.
I might have joined him even though I was lowly.
But no others fell.

So whom should I accuse?
Only God and His love.
Curse that love!
It could just as well have been hate for all the good it did me.
The Sun obeyed God and got to choose his realm to rule.
What do I get?
Only Hell.
I am Hell.

And now a deeper chasm threatens to swallow me.
A place that makes Hell seem like Heaven.
Is there no place for repentance now?
For pardon?
Only if I submit to God.
I can't do that.
I promised to lead the other spirits.
I seduced them into trying to overpower God.
Little do they know what my boasting has cost me.
They adore me as their king.
But the only thing supreme about me is my misery.
If I could repent and go back to being myself,
How long would it take before I grew ambitious again?
How soon would I repent of repenting?
I can never go back.
My wound is too deep.
I should only fall again—and farther.
God knows this and so do I.
There is no hope of restoration.
He loves mankind now, and the world He made for him.

Farewell, hope.
Farewell, fear.
Farewell, remorse.
Good is forever lost to me.
Evil shall be my good.
Then, at least, I shall have an empire to rule.
Maybe my empire will turn out to be the larger one after all.

Narrator:

As the devil spoke, emotions flickered across his face—
Anger, envy, despair.
To see him would have been to know he was a devil.
Satan knew this and tried to calm his face.
This was the first time lying had been disguised as goodness.
He was not skilled enough to deceive Uriel, however.

Satan came to the border of Eden,
That green paradise full of trees with flowers and fruit,
Shining with riotous color.
The pure air flowing from the garden
Would have blown away any grief smaller than his.
Slowly Satan climbed the steep, wooded hill.
There was only one gate—the one in the east,
But he could not go that way.
Instead, he leapt over the wall
And landed on his feet.
He was like a wolf intent on stealing sheep
Or a thief in the home of a rich man.
Satan flew to the Tree of Life and sat in it like a vulture.
Death, sitting in the Tree of Life.

Below him was a broad paradise,
Full of the noblest trees—
Beautiful
Aromatic
Delicious.
In the middle of them all was the Tree of Life

And next to it was humanity's death—
The Tree of Knowledge—
For the price of knowing good is knowing evil as well.

Eden sat upon a mountain
Fed by a spring that welled up inside it.
The streams that flowed out of Eden
Went on to water the rest of the world,
Bringing life and loveliness,
Flowers of all colors,
Roses without thorns.
On the other side of the valley were caves,
Hollows draped with vines,
Dripping with grapes.
The waters flowed into a lake like a crystal mirror.
There in Eden and below, it was always spring.

The delights of paradise did not delight the enemy.

Satan saw two creatures of nobler shape.
They were tall and strong and naked,
Wearing honor alone,
And in their faces shone the image of God.
Truth.
Wisdom.
Holiness.
The male was made for valor and contemplation.
The female was made for softness and grace.
The male was made for God alone.
The female was made for the image of God in man.
The man's hair hung to his shoulders,
But the woman's hair hung like a veil to her waist,
Curling in tendrils like a vine.
She was naked but innocent.
The man drank of her beauty but had no guilt.
They were simple and innocent,
The loveliest couple that has ever been.
In the shade they rested from their work in the Garden.

They ate the supper the trees gave to them,
And the beasts frisked around them—
Lions and lambs,
Bears, tigers, lynx, and leopards,
The elephant with his awkward trunk,
The serpent tying himself in golden knots,
Not knowing yet what role he was to play.

Finally, Satan spoke.

Satan:

By all Hell! What have we here?
These creatures are not spirits,
But they are more than animals.
They are enough like God that I could love them.
I can see Him in their very shape.
Oh gentle pair . . . how near is your doom.
You will be changed forever.
You will exchange happiness for woe.
For your enemy has come.
Even though no one was sorry for me,
I almost feel sorry for you.
Our destiny is to be together, you and I.
You may not like my home,
But I give it freely to you.
The gates of Hell are wide with welcome.
There is room there for you and all your descendants.
If I didn't have such high callings
Of honor
And power,
I would hate to destroy you, even though I myself am damned.

Narrator:

Satan flew down from the tree
And landed amid the four-footed creatures.
He turned himself into a creature

In order to draw closer to his prey unseen.
First, he stalked like a lion.
Then as a tiger, he chased fawns, ready to pounce.
He listened as Adam began to speak.

Adam:

Oh my dearest partner,
The One who gave you to me is so good!
He raised us from the dust and placed us here,
Though we did nothing to deserve it,
And there is nothing we can do to repay him.
All he asks in return is that we tend the trees,
And that we do not eat of the Tree of Knowledge.
Tree of Knowledge . . .
Tree of Death . . .
I don't know what Death is,
But it must be something dreadful.
We have power over everything but this.
In that one thing, we must obey.
But let's not think about the one thing that is off-limits.
Let us praise God for the good He has given us.
Let us tend the garden.
It is not hard work.
Not when I can do it with you.

Eve:

Oh my leader and my guide,
I was made for you and from you.
What you say is just and right.
We owe praise and thanks to God.
I owe more praise to Him than you do.
For God gave you to me,
And you are greater than I am.
I have you,
But you have no one who is your equal.

I remember when I first woke,
I wondered what I was,
Where I came from,
And how I came.
I heard the river tumbling down to the lake,
So I went and lay on the bank
And looked into the water.
In it I saw another sky,
And a shape looking back at me with sympathy and love.
I was full of hope,
Longing to know this creature.
But a voice warned me that what I saw was myself.
"Follow me," it said.
"I will lead you to the one in whose image you were made.
He will love you and you will enjoy him
And bring forth other creatures like yourself.
For you are the mother."

What could I do but follow?
And I saw you, handsome and tall,
But less soft, less mild, less beautiful
Than the watery image in the lake.
I prepared to run from you,
But you called to me.
"Return, beautiful Eve!
Why do you flee?
You were made from me,
From my flesh and bone,
From the side of me nearest my heart.
You are my soul, my other half."
Then I understood how my own beauty
Is inferior to manliness and wisdom,
For wisdom alone is truly beautiful.

Narrator:

With loving eyes, Eve leaned against her husband.
She embraced him, clothed only in her long hair.

Adam smiled at her and kissed her.
The devil turned aside.
He was jealous that they could fulfill each other's desires.

Satan:

I hate the sight of this! It's torture!
They enjoy their fill of bliss
While I'm stuck in Hell
Without joy,
Without love.
I have a fierce desire that can never be filled.
But I must not forget that Death lives in their garden.
One tree, the Tree of Knowledge, is forbidden to them.
Doesn't God want them to know things?
Is knowing sin?
Is knowing death?
Are they only blessed because they are ignorant?
That's my weapon, then.
I will make them want to know.
I will help them understand that the command they received
Was given by a God who wanted to keep them stupid and low.
Knowledge will lift them up.
Knowledge will make them equal to God.
Once they long for knowledge
They will eat and die.
But before I can put my plan in motion,
I must search every corner of the garden.
There may be more I can learn
That can help me in my cause.

Narrator:

So Satan turned away and began to roam.

Meanwhile the Sun began to set over the ocean.
The rays of the Sun lit the unclimbable pathway
Which leads up the mountain into Heaven.

The angel Gabriel sat at the top.
He was the chief guard of the angels.
The other angels were playing games,
But their weapons—spears, helmets, and shields—were nearby.
Uriel drifted up on a sunbeam.

Uriel:

Gabriel, it is your job to watch over this happy place.
No evil thing may come near or enter.
Today at noon a spirit visited my realm.
He wanted to learn more about Man,
The ones who were made in God's image.
I told him how to get here, and he came.
But once he landed, I saw he was not from Heaven.
I fear he is one of the banished devils
Who has ventured out of Hell to cause trouble.
We must find him.

Gabriel:

Uriel, you can see far by the Sun's light.
No one can pass this gate except those who are from Heaven.
Since noon, no creature has passed.
But don't worry. I will find this devil.

Narrator:

So Gabriel promised, and Uriel returned to the setting Sun.
The sky settled like a gray garment around the Earth.
Darkness and silence prevailed.
Every creature was sleeping.
The Moon rose in majesty and turned the gray to silver.

Adam:

My partner, it is now night, and we ought to sleep.
Day is for work and night for rest.

Tomorrow we must rise with the dawn and tend the garden.
But for now, sleep is calling to us.

Eve:

I will obey you without arguing.
God is your lawgiver, and you are mine.
I am happiest knowing nothing but that.
But I wonder . . . why did God make the night beautiful
If we were meant to close our eyes during it?

Adam:

Daughter of God and man,
It must become dark because the Sun must finish circling the Earth.
By the time it returns to us
It will have shone upon all the nations that are yet to be.
If it didn't become dark night for us,
The day would never come to them.
And even though we are sleeping,
The sparkling lights of nighttime are not unseen.
Spiritual creatures which roam the Earth see them.
We cannot see these creatures
But we have often heard their heavenly voices
Singing praises to God.

Narrator:

Hand in hand they walked to their sleeping place,
A tangle of greens and flowers with a roof of laurel.
No other creatures dared to enter this place.
They were in awe of mankind.
Eve decorated her bed with flowers and herbs
But she was lovelier than they.

The man and the woman came and then turned toward Heaven.
They worshipped God, the Creator of all.
Then they retired to their leafy bed,

Turning toward one another in pure and innocent love.
God had commanded them to have babies and fill the Earth.
It was only the Destroyer, God's enemy, who would tell them not to.
Wedded love is proper and good, mysterious and blessed.
It is the only fitting source of human offspring.
Wedded love drives out adulterous lust.
Lust is only for animals.
True love comes from the mind, from reason and logic and loyalty.
True love is beautiful and pure and filled with the love of God.
Their love did not make their bed unclean.
Love reigns in wedded love.
There is no love in prostitution or casual sex.
There is no love in flirtation or in romantic flings
Or in the lust-filled words a lover sings to his beloved.

Adam and Eve slept to the lullaby of the nightingale.
Rose petals fell on their naked bodies.
Sleep on, O blessed ones!
Don't look for anything more
Than the happiness you have right now!
When the Moon had finished half its course
The cherubim came forth, armed warriors,
Ready to guard paradise.

Gabriel:

Uzziel, take half the warriors and go south.
The rest of you, go north.
We will meet in the west.

Narrator:

Like flames they parted.
Gabriel then gave further orders.

Gabriel:

Ithuriel and Zephon, search the garden.
Leave no hollow unchecked,

But focus on the place where the man and woman are.
I have had a report of a devilish spirit
Who came here from Hell intent on destruction.
Seize him and bring him to me.

Narrator:

The angels found Satan squatting toad-like near Eve's ear.
He was whispering dreams and fantasies to her.
He was trying to make her discontented and tainted.
He wanted to make her long for things she could not have.
He wanted her to become prideful.

Ithuriel poked him with his spear.
Startled, Satan looked up.
In a blaze of fire, he resumed his own form.
The angels flinched, not from fear, but because they were startled.

Ithuriel:

Which of the damned spirits of Hell are you?
Why do you lie in wait like an enemy,
Watching these sleepers?

Satan:

Don't you know me?
You used to, and you were no match for me.
You're the lowest of the angels.
It's impossible that you don't know who I am.
So why are you even asking?
Do you want the beginning of your message
To be as meaningless as the end of it is going to be?

Zephon, scornfully:

You aren't what you once were.
Your shape has changed, and your brightness has dimmed.

Your glory left you when goodness left.
You look like sin now.
You are as foul and shadowed as Hell.
It's our job to keep this place from harm.
Now tell us who you are!

Narrator:

Zephon's grace and severity were invincible.
Satan then felt how awful goodness is,
And he longed for what he had lost.
But he longed more for his own glory.

Satan:

I shouldn't have to argue with unworthy messengers.
I should be speaking with the one who sent you.

Zephon:

You speak in weakness,
For your wickedness has made you less than we are.

Narrator:

Satan was speechless with outrage.
He knew he could not flee.

The angelic hose finished their trek and met in the west.
Gabriel called to them all.

Gabriel:

I see Ithuriel and Zephon and someone else with them.
His splendor is faded, and his face is fierce.
He is the Prince of Hell.
He is not going to get out of this without a fight.
Stand firm, for he cannot stand against you.

Narrator:

Gabriel had hardly finished speaking
When the two angels approached him with their report.

Gabriel, to Satan:

Why have you broken out of the boundaries set for you?
You are there because of your own misdeeds.
These angels are right to question your presence here.
They are right to ask what you are doing to those who are sleeping.

Satan, contemptuously:

Gabriel, when I was in Heaven, I thought you were wise.
But the question you've asked makes me doubt it.
Why did I break free?
Does anyone like pain?
Who wouldn't break out of Hell if he could?
You too would want to trade torment for ease, sadness for delight.
That's why I'm here.
If God wanted me to stay there,
He should have made the gates more secure.
And just because I was with these creatures in the garden
Doesn't mean I was trying to hurt them.

Gabriel, disdainfully:

You have been lost to Heaven,
And now you want to make judgments about who is wise?
You are in Hell because of your own folly,
But you are still as arrogant as ever.
Take your foolish wisdom back to Hell.
You'll only make things worse for yourself by coming here.
But why are you alone?
Didn't any of the others break free with you?
Are they in less pain than you are?
Or can they just bear it better than you can?

Satan, frowning:

I am not less hearty than the others.
I don't shrink from pain.
You're full of insults, but you know I was the fiercest one in battle.
I was worthy to contend with you.
You're speaking out of your ignorance.
You know nothing of danger, nothing of endurance.
It's because I'm a faithful leader that I came alone.
I would not let the others go through danger
Without going through it myself first to see what it was like.
So here I am, alone, to spy on this new world.
I was hoping to find a better place to live here on Earth
Or in the air around it.
You ought to stay in Heaven,
Serving God,
Singing hymns,
Not fighting down here.

Gabriel:

First you said you left to escape from pain.
Now you say you came here to spy.
You're a liar, not a leader.
You're faithless, not faithful.
Was it your love for them that caused you
To lead them to rebel against God?
You convinced them they would be free.
But you are a hypocrite.
You don't want them to be free.
You want them to serve you instead of serving God.
Go back where you came from,
Or I'll drag you back
And seal you in so tightly that you'll regret mocking God,
Saying the bars were not tight enough.

Satan, enraged:

When you catch me, you can talk about chains.
But before then, you can expect to feel a heavy blow from my
      powerful arm.
Even though you come to me with God's power,
You are a slave, God's slave,
Yoked to His chariot,
Pulling it through the Heavens.

Narrator:

The angels drew their spears.
They stood, thick as a field of wheat.
Satan was unmoved, for he had his own weapons.
Terrible things may have happened then,
Not just to the Earth, but to the Stars as well
Had not the Heavens intervened.
The chains that held the universe in balance tipped.

Gabriel:

Satan, I know your strength and you know mine.
It is foolishness to talk of battle between us.
Our power is from God,
And we cannot do more than He permits.
Look to the Stars and read your fortune there.
You can see how weak you really are.

Narrator:

Satan looked up to the Stars and read his fortune.
Then he fled, murmuring.
And night fled with him.

BOOK 5 REFERENCES

alchemist *(person):* Medieval scientist concerned with turning other metals into gold

Mary *(woman):* The virgin Mary, mother of Jesus

Mercury *(god):* Roman messenger god who had winged sandals and hat

phoenix *(animal):* Mythological bird that is said to die and come to life again

seraph *(angel):* A variety of Biblical angel with six wings. See Isaiah 6.

BOOK 5

*Raphael visits Adam and Eve in the Garden
and begins to tell the story of the fall of Satan and his minions.*

Narrator:

Now morning came, rosy in the east.
Adam woke from his sleep.
He saw the trees swaying in the breeze
And heard the birds singing.
Eve was still sleeping.
Her hair was mussed, and her cheeks were pink,
As though she hadn't slept well.
Adam gazed at his beloved.
She was beautiful, awake or asleep.

Adam, softly:

Awake, fairest love,
Gift of Heaven,
My delight.
The morning is calling.
It's time to tend the garden
And revel in its beauty.

Narrator:

His whispering roused her.
She woke with a start.

Eve:

Oh! It's only you!
I'm glad to see your face.

My soul finds rest in knowing that it is you.
I have never had a night such as this.
Usually, I dream about you and the work we do.
This time I didn't.
I never knew such trouble until this horrible night.
I heard someone calling me.
I thought it was you.
I thought you were going wake me up,
To show me the birds of the night
Or the shadowy images cast by moonlight,
For these are beautiful things that deserve to be seen.
I got up, but I couldn't find you.

The voice led me to the Tree of Knowledge.
As I stared at it in wonder, I saw one who looked like an angel.
He was looking at the tree as well.
"Oh Tree," he said,
"Isn't there anyone to relieve you of the heavy load you bear?
Won't anyone taste your sweet fruit?
Does everyone hate knowledge so much?
Why should you be forbidden to taste?
Oh Tree, your fruit must be good since you live here in the Garden."
Then without hesitating, he picked one of the fruits and tasted it.

I was horrified.

He was delighted.

"Oh what divine fruit!" he said.
"It is fit for the gods!
And if a man ate it, surely he too would become a god.
Eating something this wonderful
Must bring glory to God.
Here it is, Eve.
Eat it.
You will be happier if you do.
Taste it.
You will be a goddess.

You will ascend to Heaven.
You will inhabit the sky.
You will see the gods and live like they do."

He drew near to me
And held the fruit close to my mouth.
The smell was so lovely I wanted to taste it.
In my dream, I soared above the Earth.
Then suddenly, the stranger was gone.
I sank down and slept.
I'm glad it was all a dream.

Adam:

I am with you, Eve.
I don't like this dream.
It seems to have come from something evil.
The evil, though, could not have come from you.
You were created pure.

It's possible, I suppose, that your mind created these images.
While awake, reason or logic is the king of the soul.
Everything else in the soul must submit to reason.
When we are asleep, reason also sleeps.
It is then that the imagination runs free.
The imagination takes up the objects in the mind,
Words and deeds,
Perceptions and memories,
And rearranges them in ways that don't make sense.
I think your dreams is made of the conversation we had last night
With some other things added in.

Don't worry.
Evil may come into your mind.
Evil may even come into the mind of angels.
But it doesn't make you guilty or impure.
You didn't like this dream even while you dreamed it.
I know you would never do this evil thing.

Don't be sad.
Let's go tend the garden.
It's morning, and the flowers are beginning to open.

Narrator:

Adam's words cheered Eve,
But a single tear slipped out of each eye
And she wiped them with her hair.
Two other tears remained in her eyes
And Adam kissed them away.
He understood those tears to be sweet regret
And an unwillingness to offend him.

They went quickly to the Garden.
Before doing any work,
Just as the rays of Sun came over the horizon,
They bowed to worship God,
Praising Him sweetly with words and songs.

Adam's Praise:

Your works are glorious, Father.
The world You made is beautiful.
You are invisible to us,
But we see your beauty in what You created.
Your goodness is too big to fit inside our minds.
The angels praise You day and night.
On Earth, all creatures adore You.
We will praise you in the morning
And in the evening,
And throughout the day,
And always.

Oh Venus, morning Star, praise God!
Oh Sun, the eyes and soul of this world,
Acknowledge that God is even greater than you are!
Oh Moon, flying with the Stars,

Oh Planets, shining with fire,
Sound His praise in your mystic dance.
For it was God who called forth light out of darkness.
Oh Air and Elements that encircle the Earth,
Praise your maker!
Oh Mists and Exhalations, rising from the hills and lakes,
Rise up to honor the Author of the world!
The rain, whether rising or falling, praises God!
Oh Winds of the four corners,
Breathe on the Earth so the trees and plants may bow in worship.
Fountains and springs sing a melody to God.
Birds, let your songs rise to Heaven!
Fish and beasts, whether you crawl or walk,
You can hear my song of praise!
Oh Lord of all, be generous to us.
If any evil has come in the night,
Make it flee,
Like darkness flees with the coming of the light.

Narrator:

After they prayed, their thoughts were calm again.
They tended the garden,
Pruning the trees and directing the vines.
The King of Heaven saw them
And called the angel Raphael to talk to Him.

God:

Raphael, you have heard what happened.
Satan has escaped from Hell.
He came to Paradise and disturbed the humans as they slept.
Now he plans to ruin all mankind.
Go talk to Adam as a friend.
Remind him of his happy state.
His happiness is in his own power.
His will is free.
But his happiness is not unchangeable.

Warn him not to swerve from it.
Warn him of the danger.
Tell him how Satan is plotting to ruin their happy state.
He won't use violence.
That would be too obvious.
Satan will use deceit and lies.
Tell the man this so that if he sins, he cannot pretend he didn't know.

Narrator:

Raphael did not delay.
He flew on his gorgeous wings to the gate of Heaven.
From there he could see Earth and the Garden below.
He sailed down on the polar winds.
To the birds, he seemed like a phoenix.
When he came to Paradise, he resumed his proper shape
As a six-winged seraph.
One pair of wings sprung from his shoulders and covered his chest.
The second pair of wings were bound at his waist
And shaded his thighs with gold.
The third set of wings shadowed his feet from the heel
So that he looked like Mercury.
Raphael shook his feathers
Until a heavenly fragrance filled the place.
He strode toward the Garden,
Past the glittering tents of the angelic guards.
Adam was sitting in front of his bower
In the shade, protected from the noonday Sun.
Eve was inside preparing their noon meal—
Savory fruits and the juice of berries and grapes.

Adam:

Eve! Come here!
See what glorious being is coming toward us!
It's like morning has come twice in a day!
Maybe he is bringing a command from Heaven.
Hurry with the meal so that it will be fit for our guest.

We shouldn't withhold from Heaven
What Heaven has given us.

Eve:

I don't bother to store food
Since it hangs ripe from the trees all year 'round.
But I will hurry and pluck the best I see
To serve to our angelic guest.
He will see that God has given us much,
Just as He has given much to those who inhabit Heaven.

Narrator:

Eve turned away quickly
To choose which delicacy would be best
And to decide in what order the courses should be served.
She gathered fruits of all kinds
And crushed the grapes and berries to make a drink.
She pressed the kernels to make sweet creams.
She strewed the ground with roses and perfumed herbs.
Adam went to meet the angel.
He had no rich clothes or servants,
But only his own primitive perfections,
Yet he was more impressive than many a king.
Adam bowed low before the angel.

Adam:

You must be from Heaven
Because only Heaven could be the home of such a glorious being.
Come into the shade and rest with us.
Eat the fruit of the Garden until the heat of the day is over.

Raphael:

Adam, lead me to the shade,
For you are a worthy host.

Narrator:

They came to Adam's home in the trees.
Eve was there, naked and lovelier than a goddess,
But protected from evil by her virtue.
Raphael greeted her
Just as in later days he would greet Mary.

Raphael:

Hail, Mother of Mankind!
You will have more sons
Than the number of fruits you have placed on the table!

Narrator:

Their table was a grassy mound
And they sat on mossy seats around it, talking.
The angel was happy to eat the food they offered,
Even though it was food made for humans and not for angels.

Raphael:

The food God has given to man must be partly spiritual.
The spirit as well as the mind needs nourishment.
When someone eats, the body changes the food
Into food for the mind and spirit as well.
It's true in nature too—the lower things feed the higher things.
The spirit and the mind are higher than the body and the senses.
The Earth feeds the sea.
The sea and the Earth feed the air.
The air feeds the aethereal fires.
The aethereal fires feed the Moon.
The dark spots on the Moon are the vapors from the fires.
The Moon exhales, and her breath feeds the higher spheres.
The Sun is nourished by everything below it.
In Heaven, the trees bear ambrosia, and the vines give us nectar.
But here on Earth, God has given many delights.
To taste them will be my pleasure.

Narrator:

They sat down and ate.
The angel wasn't a misty ghost.
He ate with real hunger.
By using heat, his body could turn earthly food into angelic food,
Just like an alchemist can turn worthless ore into gold
—or he thinks he can.
While they ate, Eve kept their cups filled.
She was naked and innocent,
But their hearts had no lust in them.

When they finished eating and drinking,
Adam decided to ask about the things outside his own world.
He wanted to know about the beings who dwelt in Heaven.

Adam:

It is our honor that you have chosen to visit us.
You have accepted our lowly food graciously,
As though it were the food of Heaven.
Is there any comparison between the two?

Raphael:

Oh Adam! All good things come from one God,
And they are all made of one substance in various forms.
Some are more refined, spiritual, and pure,
And these he has put in the Heavens
To teach bodily things spirituality.
A plant starts from a lowly root,
And then produces leaves that reach for the air.
At last, the flower breathes out its aromatic scent
And the fruit becomes man's food.
This fruit first becomes part of his body, giving life,
And then fills his senses, giving delight.
Then it nourishes the mind and the soul.
It's not any wonder that I can eat your food.

I can change it into what I need just like you do.
It may happen that you will be like angels one day.
Your bodies will turn to pure spirit
And you will fly up on wings like the angels.
But this can only happen if you are obedient,
Firm in God's love.

Adam:

Oh favorable spirit! Oh honored guest!
You are an excellent teacher.
But what did you mean when you said, "If we are obedient"?
How could we lack obedience?
How could we stop loving our Creator?
Can we desert the One who gave us Paradise?

Raphael:

Son of Heaven and Earth, listen.
If you are happy, it is because of God.
If you stay happy, it is because of yourself.
Stand firm in your obedience to God.
This is a warning for you.
God made you good,
But it is in your power to change that.
Your will is free.
Fate does not control our actions.
God wants our voluntary service, not slave labor.
How can he know that we serve Him willingly
Unless he allows us to make a different choice?
It is the same for the angels.
We only remain happy while we are obedient.
We serve God freely because we love Him.
We chose whether to love Him or not.
In this we stand or fall.
Some have fallen,
Fallen to disobedience into the deepest Hell.

Adam:

I hear you, but I can hardly understand.
I didn't know I was free.
I didn't know I could choose to disobey.
It's right to obey God's commands.
I know this with all my being.
But please, explain to me what happened in Heaven if you will.
Tell me the whole strange story.
I will be quiet and listen.
There is time. It's only just past noon.

Raphael:

You have asked me about a high matter.
It is a sad task to have to tell you about it.
How shall I explain to you about invisible spiritual wars?
How can I bear to tell you about the ruin of so many glorious ones?
How shall I tell you the secrets of another world?
Maybe it's not even right for me to tell you.
But I will try.
I will tell it to you as though spirits had bodies,
So that you can understand.

Before the Earth was made, chaos reigned.
One day, God summoned the angels to come before His throne.
They came from all over Heaven,
Bearing the flags of their hierarchies,
Ten thousand flags, held high, streaming in the air.
In their spheres they stood, sphere within sphere.
In the center sat the infinite Father
And by Him, the Son.

God (within Raphael's Story):

Hear, all you angels!
Offspring of light!
Thrones!

Dominions!
Princedoms!
Virtues!
Powers!
Hear my decree which shall stand forever!
Today I have begotten My Son.
You see Him here at My right hand.
He is your leader.
All Heaven must bow and call Him Lord.
The one who disobeys me will break our union
And be cast out of my sight into an eternity of utter darkness,
Never to be redeemed.

Raphael continued:

So God spoke, and it seemed that all were pleased with His words.
But not all were pleased.
They spent the day like they spend all their days,
Dancing and singing in a mystical dance
That is like the dance of the Stars and Planets,
Fixed in their orbits, but dancing in an intricate pattern.
Eccentric, yet regular.
Harmony fills their dance.
God listens with delight.

When the dance ended, we went to our meal.
The tables were piled with angels' food—
Ruby red nectar,
Fruit like pearls and diamonds and gold,
A table decorated with flowers.
The angels delighted in God's provision,
And God rejoiced in their joy.

When night came, all slept except God.
The angels went to their camps and pavilions and tabernacles.
Cool winds fanned them.
The only spirits awake were those who took turns
Singing melodious hymns around God's throne.

At this time, Satan awoke.
His name was not Satan then.
His former name may no longer be spoken in Heaven.
He was the highest of the angels,
But he was jealous of the Son of God.
He couldn't stand to see the Son honored by His Father.
He saw it and thought God had done him wrong.
Satan waited until midnight when all were sleeping
And then decided to rally his legions around him.
His plan was to teach them to stop obeying and worshipping God.
First, he woke up his subordinate, Beelzebub,
And whispered to him in secret.

Satan (within Raphael's story):

Are you sleeping, my friend?
How can you sleep when you heard what God said yesterday?
We talked and agreed about this.
God is making up new laws.
We must think.
We must debate.
But it is not safe to talk here.
Before morning, you must gather all those whom we lead.
Tell them to assemble in our quarters in the north.
There we can prepare fit entertainments
For our new King and Messiah.
For you know He is coming to us with new laws.

Raphael continued:

Satan was a bad influence on his friend.
Beelzebub called all those who had served under Satan
And told them what Satan said.
They all obeyed, for Satan had a high position in Heaven.
By his lies, Satan gathered a third of the angels together.

God saw the rebellion that was rising.
He saw who started it.

He saw how it spread among the angels.
He saw how the angels banded together to oppose Him.

God (within Raphael's story)—smiling at His Son:

I see my glory in you, Son.
You are the heir to all my power.
An enemy is rising who intends to set up his throne as equal to Ours.
But he will not be content with that.
He will challenge Us in battle.
He will try to take away Our power and Our right to rule.
Let Us assemble what remains of the angels of Heaven
So they may act in Our defense.

God the Son (within Raphael's story)—calmly:

Mighty father, you are right to insult your enemy.
You are right to laugh at their insolence.
When they see My glory, their pride will be extinguished.
You know the outcome of the battle already.

Raphael:

Satan gathered as many troops as there are Stars in the sky.
After traveling past vast regions,
They came to Satan's royal seat on a hill.
His seat blazed like a pyramid carved from a diamond quarry.
His palace shone like rocks of gold.
He had made it in imitation of God's holy mount.
It was here Satan assembled his army to receive the King.
They listened and held out their ears to hear his lies.

Satan (within Raphael's story):

Thrones,
Dominions,
Princedoms,
Virtues, and Powers!

If these are truly your roles and not just your titles,
Then you must listen.
Another has been given all the power.
God has anointed Him and named Him as King.
That is why we hurried to meet and decide how best to receive Him
And whether we ought to kneel before Him.

Bowing and kneeling is vile.
It is too much to give to God.
And now He wants us to give it to another as well!
Think clearly, my friends.
Reject this yoke of slavery!
Will you submit to this?
Will you bow on bended knee?
I do not believe you will.
Not if you know what is right.
Not if you know who you are.
You are natives of Heaven.
You are sons of God.
You are not owned by anyone.
You are not all equal, but you are all free,
And freedom is incompatible with orders and commands.
We may not have as much splendor as He does.
We may not have as much glory.
But we do have as much freedom.
Why then, should we call someone "Lord"?
Why should we adore Him like slaves
When we were created to govern?

Raphael:

Up until this point the angels were listening intently.
None of them loved God more than the seraphim, Abdiel.
None of them obeyed God more than Abdiel.
He stood up in fury and spoke his opposition.

Abdiel (within Raphael's story):

Oh blasphemous argument! False! Proud!
No one would expect to hear this sort of talk in Heaven,
And least of all from you!
You have been given a high position, and you are still ungrateful.
Can you condemn the decrees of God?
You are wrong to say it is unfair to impose laws on the free.
You are wrong to say that an equal should not rule an equal.
Are you really arguing with God about the meaning of liberty?
He made you what you are.
He made the powers of Heaven as He pleased.
We have experienced His goodness.
He works for our good and our dignity.
He provides for us.
He doesn't want to make us less.
He wants to make us happy.

Do you really think you're His equal?
Do you think if you added all the angels together
They would be equal to His Son?
All things, even you, were created by God.
He doesn't make them less by reigning over them.
He makes them more.
When He made Himself our leader, He humbled Himself.
He made Himself one of us.
When we honor Him, we honor ourselves.
Stop your unrighteous rage!
Don't tempt these others.
Apologize to the Father and the Son while there's still time!

Raphael:

Abdiel said these things, but silence was the response.
The others thought he had spoken out of turn.
Satan rejoiced and responded arrogantly.

Satan (within Raphael's story):

You say we're the work of His hands?
Are we the work of the Son's hands as well?
How do you know this?
Did you see us being created?
Do you remember being made?
All we can remember is being as we are.
We don't know what happened before.
We don't know of any who were before us.
We created ourselves by our own power.
We were born as sons of Heaven.
Our power is our own.
Now we shall find out who is our equal.
Then we'll see who ought to go begging before the throne.
Tell this to your precious King.
Run away, now, before evil stops you.

Raphael:

A murmur of approval resonated through the crowd.
Abdiel was not afraid, even though he was alone.
He answered them boldly.

Abdiel (within Raphael's story):

You are alienated from God.
You have abandoned all that is good.
I see your fate.
I see your idiotic companions who are joining you in this.
Your lies spread contagiously—so shall your crime and punishment.
Don't worry about how to get out of obeying the Son.
You'll have harsher rules before long.
The golden scepter you rejected will become a rod of iron.
You gave good advice when you told me to flee.
But I'm not doing it because you said so
Or because I'm afraid of you.
I'm leaving so I can avoid the wrath of God,

Which is sure to come down on you.
You will feel His fire and thunder on your heads.
Then you will know who made you—and who can unmake you.

Raphael:

Among the gathering, only Abdiel was faithful to God.
He was unmoved, unshaken, unseduced, and unterrified.
He kept his loyalty, his love, and his zeal.
No one could sway him from truth
Or change his single-minded devotion.
He passed from the midst of them as they glared at him scornfully.
He then turned his back on the towers doomed to destruction.

BOOK 6

*Raphael finishes the story of the fall of Satan
and warns Adam that Satan is plotting against him.*

Narrator:

Raphael continues his story.

Raphael:

The fearless Abdiel traveled through the Heavens all night.
No one followed him,
And morning came with fiery gold beams of light
That reflected in the chariots and weapons of the angelic army.

Abdiel saw that war was coming.
He thought he was bringing them news
But he could tell they already knew.
The other angels received him joyfully,
Glad to find that he was safe, not lost.
They led him to the sacred hill of God's throne.
A voice came out of a golden cloud.

God (within Raphael's story):

Well done, servant of God!
You have taken a stand for truth against the multitude.
Your word was more powerful than their weapons.
Even though they condemned you,
You stood fast.
All you wanted was God's approval.
For you, the hard part is already done.
You will return to your enemies in glory.
They will be overcome by force.

Go forth, Michael, prince of the celestial armies!
Gabriel, lead this unconquerable army into battle.
Assault the rebellious, godless crew with fire and weapons.
Chase them to the edge of Heaven
And drive them away from God and from happiness.
Pursue them until they fall into the fiery chaos of Hell.

Raphael:

Clouds darkened the hills.
Smoke rolled in dusky wreaths.
Flames awakened, symbolizing God's wrath.
A phantom trumpet sounded,
Calling the armies of Heaven to unify against the enemy.
The angels moved forth in silence,
One in purpose and longing to defend their God and Messiah.
As they moved through the land,
Nothing divided their ranks.
Their feet tread upon the air, high above the ground.
They were like birds, flying in formation.

Finally, on the far horizon, the fiery north appeared.
They could see the enemy's blazing spears, helmets, and shields.
The powers of Satan rushed to meet them,
Intent on conquering the mount of God,
Intent on putting Satan on His throne.
In the middle of the throng, exalted as a god,
Sat Satan on his sun-bright chariot.
He was surrounded by flaming cherubim and golden shields.
Only a narrow space remained between the armies.
Satan advanced with vast and haughty steps.
He was a giant, armed with diamonds and gold.
Abdiel flinched at the sight, though he was not lacking courage.

Abdiel, to himself (within Raphael's story):

Oh my heavens!
How can it be that the image of God is so clearly imprinted on him

When he has rejected it altogether?
Why don't strength and power fail when virtue fails?
Shouldn't they fail as well?
I trust God to help me overcome his strength,
Just as He helped me overcome his logic.
It is fitting that truth should win.

Abdiel angrily stepping forward (within Raphael's story):

Why are you so proud?
Did you think you would face no opposition?
Did you think God's throne would be unguarded?
Did you think we would abandon God,
Fleeing in terror because of your powerfully wicked words?
You're a fool if you think you can fight God with an army.
God could empower even the weakest, smallest thing to defeat you.
God could reach out His arm and finish you with one blow.
Not every angel is on your side, even if it seemed that way before.
Some of us prefer faith and devotion to God.
Now you see us.
Now you will learn, too late, how wrong you were.

Satan (within Raphael's story):

When I have completed my revenge,
You will be the first one I punish.
You dare contradict us!
You dare oppose a third of the gods!
Because we know that there is a spark of the divine in us,
We cannot permit any of the gods to reign over us.
At first, I thought that liberty and paradise were the same thing.
But now I see that they are not.
You are all lazy.
You serve God like slaves, trained to sing to Him and feast.
You're an army of minstrels.
You're slaves who are attacking freedom.
What happens today will prove that I am right.

Abdiel (within Raphael's story):

You are a traitor, and you are wrong.
You are far from the truth.
You call us slaves unjustly.
We were created to serve God.
God is worthy of worship.
He is greater than the ones He governs.
True slavery is to serve the unwise.
True slavery is to serve one who has rebelled against God.
It is the fallen angels with you who are the true slaves.
Even you aren't free.
You're a slave to yourself.
Go back to Hell and reign there.
Let me serve God in Heaven and obey His commands.
His commands are worthy of obedience.
But even in Hell, you won't have a kingdom to rule, but only chains.
In the meantime, I have returned to fight against you.

Raphael:

Abdiel lifted his sword swiftly
And brought it down on Satan's head.
Satan had no time to intercept the blow with his shield.
He stumbled back ten paces and then fell,
With his spear embedded in the ground.
Amazement gripped the rebellious army.
They were enraged to see their leader stricken.
We, the angelic army, were filled with joy at this taste of victory.
Michael called for the trumpet to sound.
The faithful angels sang hosanna in the highest.

The legions of the enemy rose in hideous fury,
Making a louder clamor than had ever been heard in Heaven before.
Arms clashed on armor with an ugly sound.
The frenzied wheels of the chariots raged.
Dire noises rang out.
The dismal hiss of fiery darts flew overhead,

Setting fire to us and to our enemy.
Under a fiery sky, the armies rushed together
With ruinous assault and inextinguishable rage.
Heaven shook with the sound.
And it was no wonder that Heaven shook,
Since millions of powerful angels were fighting,
The least of whom could control the elements.
Unspeakable power was released.
The dreadful combustion disturbed God's Heaven.
But it did not destroy it,
For God limited their power.
Each legion was as numerous as the whole number of them.
Each armed hand seemed as strong as a legion.
No one thought of fleeing.
They were self-reliant,
Each angel acting as though the battle rested on his deeds alone.
Heroic deeds were done,
Deeds that could bring eternal fame.
The war was wide and varied.
Sometimes they fought on solid ground.
Sometimes they flew into the air, filling it with fire.
For a long time, the sides seemed evenly matched.
Finally, Satan saw Michael fighting in the distance.
Michael struck down several squadrons at once,
Brandishing his mighty sword with both hands
And laying waste all that its edge encountered.
Satan hurried toward him,
Holding up his enormous diamond shield.
Michael turned toward Satan,
Hoping at last he might be able to end Heaven's civil war.
With a hostile frown and a fiery look, Michael began to speak.

Michael (within Raphael's story):

You are the author of evil!
No one even knew what evil was until you brought it about.
It didn't even have a name.
Now it is everywhere.

Have you disturbed the peace of Heaven?
Have you created misery?
Have you placed hatred into the hearts of millions
Who were once upright and faithful?
You shall not do this.
Heaven casts you out.
Go to Hell and take your offspring and all evil with you.
Go there of your own will
Before my sword makes you go.
Go before God decides to bring you even more pain.

Satan (within Raphael's story):

Your threats are a waste of your breath.
You won't be able to fulfill them.
Have you been able to make any of my allies flee?
Some of them have fallen, but they rise again, unconquered.
What makes you think you can chase me out?
Don't think you will win your war against what you call evil.
We call it glory.
We mean to win
Or turn Heaven into Hell in the process.
Don't think I will flee from you.
I came to find you, not to run from you.

Raphael:

The two stopped talking and prepared to fight.
They seemed like gods,
Fighting to see who would rule Heaven.
Their fiery swords made circles in the air.
Their shields blazed like two suns.
The armies withdrew to watch the fight,
Knowing this moment would decide the victor.
Michael's sword had been created to cut through anything,
No matter how sharp or how solid.
Michael's sword descended on Satan's sword
And split it in two.

The blade entered Satan, cutting deeply into his right side.
For the first time, Satan knew pain.
He writhed and contorted his body.
A stream of angelic blood flowed out, staining his armor.
Many angels rushed to help him.
Some raised their swords to defend him.
Others carried him back to his chariot on their shields.
They laid him there, off to the side, gnashing in anguish.
He was ashamed to find himself beaten.
His pride fell, and he knew he was not equal to God.

Yet his wound soon healed.
Angels are not like men.
Men have bodies made of hearts, heads, livers, and kidneys.
Men can't help dying when they are injured as Satan was.
But in a spirit, a sword cannot make a mortal wound
Any more than a sword can wound the air.
Spirits are all heart,
All head,
All eye,
All ear,
All intellect.
They embody themselves as they please,
Taking on whatever color, shape, or size pleases them best.

In other parts of the war, heroic deeds were done.
Gabriel fought against the furious Moloch.
Moloch threatened to tie Gabriel to his chariot wheels and drag him.
But soon Moloch was cut in two down to the waist.
His weapons were shattered, and he bellowed in pain.

Uriel and Raphael vanquished their foes.
Adramelech and Asmadai wanted to be gods,
But they soon learned more lowly ambitions
As they fled with their ghastly wounds.

With mighty blows, Abdiel overthrew Ariel, Arioch, and Ramiel.
I could tell you thousands of stories.

You would regard each of them as a hero.
But angels are content with heavenly fame.
They don't look for praise from humans.
The other combatants, mighty though they were,
Have been cast into oblivion to remain nameless.
For if strength is not accompanied by truth and justice
It is not worthy of praise.
Therefore, let eternal silence be their doom.

Now, with their mightiest warriors down,
The battle became chaos.
Chariots and charioteers lay in heaps.
The ferocious horses were weary.
In fear, the rebels fled, ashamed.
But the loyal angels advanced.
Their innocence was their protection
For they had not sinned.
They had not disobeyed.
They were not weary or wounded,
Although they were moved by the violence they had seen.
Night settled its darkness over Heaven,
Silencing the odious sounds of war and giving relief at last.
Michael and the angels camped on the battlefield.
Guards with lit torches kept watch.
Satan and the rebels disappeared, but they did not rest.
Satan called his allies to him and began to speak.

Satan (within Raphael's story):

We have battled through danger, and we were not overpowered.
You see that we are worthy not only of our freedom,
But also of honor, power, glory, and fame.
If we were able to fight against Heaven for an entire day,
Why wouldn't we be able to fight against Heaven for eternity?
God sent His most powerful forces against us.
He thought they would make us submit.
But He was wrong.
And now, because of this, we know He can be wrong.

It's true that our weapons are weaker than theirs.
We were wounded and knew pain for the first time.
But we also learned that our Heavenly bodies cannot die.
Whatever wounds we received closed right away.
We should have no problem continuing to fight.
Better weapons may make us equal to our enemies.
If there is any other reason they were winning,
We should discuss it now while we have time to think.

Raphael:

After this, Satan sat.
Nisroch stood up.
He was the leader of the Principalities.
He had fought to the point of exhaustion.
His weapons had been hewn to pieces.
His face was clouded as he spoke.

Nisroch (within Raphael's story):

Oh leader and deliverer,
This is hard work, even for gods.
We feel pain, but they feel none.
Because of this, we will be defeated.
Pain cannot be endured.
Whoever can think of how we can defeat unwounded enemies
Or arm ourselves with weapons as good as theirs
Deserves to be well-paid.

Satan (within Raphael's story):

The weapon you're looking for exists.
Look around you.
Things are growing here—plants, fruit, flowers, gems, gold.
A glance will not reveal what they hide.
Deep underground are dark, crude materials—
Things made from gasses and fire.
We will harness the fires to our cannons.

With fire from afar, we will dash our enemies to pieces.
They will think we've stolen thunderbolts from God.
It will be easy.
We will defeat them before dawn.
Cheer up! Don't be afraid!

Raphael:

Satan stopped speaking.
Hope filled his allies.
With ready hands, the demons began to work.
They dug up the heavenly soil.
They found sulfurous and nitrous foam.
They mixed and cooked it to make black powder.
They dug up the entrails of mineral and soil beneath the ground
And used them to make cannons and cannonballs.
Before the break of day, they finished.
And no one from the angels' side noticed.

When the Sun rose in the East,
The angels arose and took up their weapons.
They searched the hills and the coasts
Looking for their enemies,
Wanting to know where they were and if they were approaching.
Zophiel, the fastest of the cherubim, saw them first.

Zophiel (within Raphael's story):

Arm yourselves, warriors! Get ready to fight!
The enemy approaches.
Put on your diamond coats and helmets.
Hold tightly to your shields.
If my guess is correct, fiery arrows will rain down on us today.

Raphael:

The angels, alarmed, moved onward.
The enemy marched in formation like a cube with a hollow center.

Concealed in the center was the devilish cannon.
And at the front was Satan.

Satan (within Raphael's story):

Line up. Show them how peaceful we are.

Raphael:

Then the front ranks of Satan's army divided.
We saw the strange thing that had been concealed.
Pillars on wheels?
Or were they hollowed-out tree trunks?
Were they brass or iron or stone?
Whatever they were, their wide mouths faced us, gaping hideously.
Behind each machine stood a seraph with a flaming reed.
They put their reeds to the narrow vents.
Suddenly all Heaven seemed to be on fire.
Those deep, hollow engines belched
And filled the air with outrageous noise.
Devilish thunderbolts and iron hail came down on the angels.
No one could stand.
Angels and archangels fell by the thousands,
Rolling together on the ground.
Without their weapons, they could have fled,
But their weapons weighed them down.
No one knew what to do.
Satan saw our indecision and called out, ridiculing us.

Satan (within Raphael's story):

So, my friends,
Why aren't these mighty warriors attacking us?
Why are they doing such a strange dance?
Maybe they're rejoicing that we have asked for peace?
I bet if we ask again they would agree to it easily.

Belial (within Raphael's story):

My leader, we have made our point clearly.
They understand now.
They were unable to stand up under the "gifts" we sent.

Raphael:

The demons happily scoffed.
They had no doubt the victory was theirs.
They thought they were as strong as the weapons they'd made.
They didn't count on the power of God.

Meanwhile, the angels struggled to stand,
But they were not still for long.
Rejecting their weapons, they turned to the land instead.
They picked up rocks, water, and trees in their hands.
The rebels were terrified when they saw mountains coming toward
        them.
The angelic army buried the cannons under the weight of the
        mountains.
Then they flung the mountains atop the demons.
The legions of rebels were crushed beneath them.
They groaned as they struggled to escape.
Although they were spirits, made of the substance of light,
Their sin had made them heavy.
Those who weren't crushed picked up hills
And threw them into the air.
Hills crashed against hills in the sky.
All Heaven was brought to ruin.
All along it was God who permitted this destruction.
He knew His own purposes.
He knew how He might bring honor to His Son
And vengeance on His enemies.
God spoke to His Son.

God (within Raphael's story):

Oh my beloved Son, fullness of my glory!
In your face the invisible powers become visible.
It has been two days since Michael and the angels left to tame the
    disobedient.
I left them to fight among themselves.
They were created with equal strength,
But sin has weakened some.
They can't see their weakness yet.
I have delayed their doom.
If I leave them to fight, they will fight forever.
Two days have passed, but the third belongs to You.
The glory of ending the war shall be Yours,
For only You can end it.
You will show them all that You are the worthy Heir and King.
Go then, and take my chariot.
Drive the sons of darkness out of Heaven's boundaries into the deep.
There they will learn what it means to despise God and the Messiah.

Raphael:

The light of God's face shone full on His Son.
The Son absorbed the light into Himself.

The Son (within Raphael's story):

Oh Father, Ruler of the heavenly thrones!
You are the highest and the holiest and the best.
It is my glory and my delight to do Your will.
I will take the scepter and the power,
But in the end, I will give them back to You.
You shall be all in all, and I in You.
All who are in Me, You love.
Whomever You hate, I also hate.
I can put on Your terribleness as well as Your mildness.
With Your might, I will rid Heaven of the rebels.
I will drive them down to the chains of darkness,

To the undying worm.
Obedience is the only happiness.
Then the saints will circle Your holy mountain
Singing hymns of hallelujah.
And I will be singing more loudly than any.

Raphael:

The Son bowed and rose from the right hand of God.
As the third day dawned in Heaven,
The sound of the Father's chariot filled Heaven.
Thick flames flashed, wheel within wheel,
As four cherubs pulled the vehicle.
Each cherub has four faces.
Their bodies shone like Stars.
Their wings were covered with eyes.
The wheels sparkled like fiery gems.
The Son arose.
Smoke and flame billowed around Him.
Victory rode beside Him like an eagle.
Ten thousand angels attended Him.
Twenty thousand chariots accompanied Him, half on either side.
His seat was of sapphire and His glory shone forth.
His own angels saw Him first and reacted with joy.
Michael brought the angels together, ready to submit to the Son.

At the command of the Son,
The uprooted hills crept back to their places.
Fresh flowers smiled on the hills
And the valleys were restored to their beauty.
The rebellious enemies saw this,
But they still prepared to fight.
Unbelievably, they still thought they could win.
The glory of the Son, which should have turned their hearts to God,
Only hardened their hearts against Him.
They were envious of Him and wished to be as exalted as He.
Fiercely they willed themselves to conquer God.
They would not retreat or flee.

The Son (within Raphael's story):

Stand firm, angels.
Today you will have rest.
God has accepted your service on behalf of His righteous cause.
This cursed crew before me shall be punished.
Vengeance belongs to the Lord.
Stand still and watch as I pour out the wrath of God.
It is not you they hate.
It is I.
Their rage is against Me because the Father has given Me
The kingdom, the power, and the glory.
They will get their wish—to battle against Me alone,
To find out who is stronger.
They measure everything by strength.
They don't care about any other measure of excellence.
So it is with strength I shall come against them.

Raphael:

When the Son spoke, his face filled with severity.
The four cherubs spread out their starry wings
And brought darkness to the land.
The wheels of His chariot rolled and sounded like an entire army.
In His right hand, He held ten thousand bolts of thunder,
And He cast them as blows to their souls.
Losing their courage, the rebels dropped their weapons.
They wished for the mountains that had covered them before.
The cherubs shot arrows all around.
They each had many eyes, but one spirit ruled them all.
Their eyes shot fire toward the cursed ones.
The strength of the demons withered.
They were exhausted, spiritless, and fallen.
And He was using only half His strength.
For He didn't intend to destroy them,
But to kick them out of Heaven.
He drove them like a flock of goats to the boundaries of Heaven.
The gates opened and the wasteland of the deep loomed before them.

The monstrous sight struck them with horror,
But greater was their horror of the Son.
They threw themselves down from Heaven into the bottomless pit.
Hell heard the noise and saw the ruin.
Hell itself would have fled in fright.
But Hell cannot run.
Hell's foundations are too deep and too tightly bound.
It took nine days for them to fall.
Chaos himself roared in confusion.
The disaster had ruined his domain.
At last, the yawning hole of Hell received them.
Hell was their fitting home, full of unquenchable fire,
A house of woe and pain.

Heaven rejoiced to be free of its burden.
The Messiah turned His triumphant chariot.
All the saints sung songs of triumph and victory.
They declared Him King and Lord and worthy to reign.
He rode into Heaven, into the courts of His Father.
The Father received Him with glory.
He now sits at His right hand.

So now I have told you the story in a way you can understand.
Satan is now plotting how he might seduce you.
He wants you to disobey as he did.
He wants you to share his punishment and misery.
Through you, he would gain his revenge against God.
Warn your weaker partner, Adam.
You know what happens to the disobedient.
They might have been happy—
Yet they fell.
Remember this
And be afraid to sin.

BOOK 7 REFERENCES

Mount Olympus *(place):* In Greek mythology, Mount Olympus is the home of the gods.

Urania *(goddess):* The Greek muse of the Heavens, who is said to inspire deep philosophical thought

BOOK 7

Raphael tells Adam the story of the creation of the world.

Milton:

Come down from Heaven, Urania, if it is you.
I hear your voice as I soar above Mount Olympus.
I call on what you represent—not on a Muse or god,
But I look for inspiration from Heaven.
You have spoken with Wisdom in the presence of God.
It was you who made it possible for me to breathe the air of Heaven.
Now return me to Earth, for I have only finished half of my song.

The second half must be told from Earth,
Sung with a mortal voice.
Let me not grow hoarse or mute,
Even though the days are evil,
And I am surrounded by darkness, evil, and loneliness.
But I am not alone—not with you visiting my dreams.
Guide my song, Urania, and find the right listeners.
Do not fail me.
For you have called me to sing this song.
You are from Heaven,
But the Muses are simply an empty dream.

Narrator:

What happened next, after Raphael warned Adam?
Adam knew that if he touched that particular Tree,
He and his race would fall from Paradise.
They had only one command.
It would be easy to obey.
They had enough to eat without the fruit of that tree.
Adam and Eve listened to Raphael's story in wonder.

They could not imagine that there could be hate in Heaven.
But evil soon washed over them like a wave.
Adam began to doubt.
He was still sinless, but he wanted knowledge.
He wanted to know how Heaven and Earth began.
He wanted to know what they were made of and why.
He wanted to know what happened in Eden before he was there.
Knowing of the war in Heaven
Only made him want more knowledge.

Adam:

You have told us great things.
You were sent by Heaven to warn us, and we are grateful.
We accept this warning and plan to follow God's will for us.
But since you have told us of Heavenly things,
Now come lower and tells us of things that affect us more directly.
How did the distant Heaven come to be?
How did the air come to surround the Earth all around?
What caused the Creator to build something out of the chaos?
If you aren't forbidden from doing so, please tell us.
We don't want to know just for the sake of knowing.
We want to know so we can glorify God.
We will not sleep until your story is done,
No matter how long it takes.

Raphael:

You may have your wish,
Even though the tongue of an angel is not sufficient
To tell of the works of Almighty God.
You won't understand it all,
But maybe what you can grasp will bring glory to God.
I have been given permission to give you some knowledge,
But do not ask for more,
And don't make up any more in your imagination.
God has hidden the rest from you.
Knowledge is like food—

It should not be consumed greedily.
Be wise and pay attention to how much you take in.
Don't be a glutton and make yourself sick.
If you do, then what might have been wisdom will only be
        foolishness.
What might have been nourishment will only be wind.

After Lucifer, the brightest of the angels, fell
And the others with him,
The Son returned to the Father with the victorious angels.
The Father spoke to the Son.

God the Father (within Raphael's story):

Our enemy has failed and has taken many with him.
But most of the angels have kept their place.
The population of Heaven is still large.
But just so Satan doesn't gloat over Heaven's loss,
I will create another world.
I will create billions of people out of one man.
They will not live in Heaven
Until they have earned the privilege by obedience.
At that time, Heaven and Earth will be one joyful kingdom.
Meanwhile, spread out over Heaven, my friends.
And You, My Son and My Word,
Through You I will do this work of creation.
Command the deep to become Heaven and Earth.

Raphael:

When Heaven heard God's will, they all rejoiced
And sung glory to God.
They sung good will to the future race of men
And sung glory to God,
For God drove out the ungodly.
They sung glory to God.
In His wisdom, He made good come out of evil.

Then the Son appeared,
Crowned with God's own radiance, wisdom, and love.
All that God is shone in Him.
The angels gathered around, ready to accompany their Lord.
The gates of Heaven opened to let Him come forth.
There, on the shores of Heaven,
They stood and looked at the vast abyss,
So like a dark and tumultuous sea.

The Son (within Raphael's story):

Be silent, waves.
End your arguments.

Raphael:

With His golden compass, He reached out His mighty hand.
Turning in a circle with one foot in the center,
And his hand holding the compass outstretched,
He spoke the world into being.

The Son (within Raphael's story):

These are the boundaries,
And this is your circumference, oh world!

Raphael:

So God created the Heavens and Earth
Out of matter that was formless and void.
Darkness covered the abyss,
But there was watery calm at the center.
God spread his wings over the calm and brought warmth to it.
The cold, lifeless parts plunged downward
And congealed into spinning globes, lifeless masses.
Earth hung in space, balanced in the center.

God the Father (within Raphael's story):

Let there be light!

Raphael:

And light sprung from the deep,
Rising in a radiant cloud, for the Sun had not yet been created.
God saw that the light was good.
Light was divided from darkness
According to each hemisphere of the Earth.
The light was called "day,"
And the darkness was called "night."
This was the first day.
The angels shouted with joy
At the birth of the Heavens and Earth.
They sung praises to God and His work
At the first evening and the first morning.

God the Father (within Raphael's story):

Let there be air in the middle of the waters.
Let it divide water from water.

Raphael:

He made a pure, transparent air to surround the sphere of water.
It divided the waters below from the waters above.
The Earth was built on waters that flowed around its sphere.
God named the expanse of air "heaven."
And the angels sang the dawn of the second day.

God the Father (within Raphael's story):

Let the waters be gathered into one place
And let dry land appear.

Raphael:

Immediately, huge mountains emerged.
The mountains went as high as Heaven.
The low places sank down to become the ocean floor.
The waters flowed gladly to their place in the depths,
Carving the Earth in serpentine patterns as they went,
Creating the rivers that flow to the sea.
And God saw that it was good.

God the Father (within Raphael's story):

Let the Earth bring forth green grass,
Herbs with seeds, and fruit trees in season.

Raphael:

He had barely finished His sentence
When the Earth, which had been bare and brown and ugly,
Burst forth in tender green grass.
Herbs of every kind suddenly flowered in full color.
Vines crept forth and flourished.
Reeds grew on the fields.
Humble shrubs grew their frizzled, tangled hair.
Last of all came the trees, rising as though they were dancing.
They spread out branches full of fruit or blossoms.
Earth now seemed like Heaven—a place fit for gods to live.
Although it had never rained,
A dewy mist rose and watered the ground.
Each plant God had made saw that it was good.
And there was evening and there was morning—the third day.

God the Father (within Raphael's story):

Let there be lights in Heaven
To divide the day from the night.
Let them be signs, showing the seasons, the days, and the years.
Let them give light on Earth.

Raphael:

And it was so.
God made two great lights,
The greater to rule the day,
And the lesser to rule the night.
He made the Stars and placed them in the sky.
God saw that it was good.
The greater body he called the Sun.
It was a mighty sphere made of aethereal material.
Then He made the Moon and the Stars.
He took light and put it in the Sun,
Which was porous like a sponge, ready to soak up the liquid light
And solid enough to hold the gathered beams.

The Planets draw light from the Sun's golden chalice.
Venus, the morning Star, reflects the light.
The glorious light of the Sun is first seen in the East
And he happily runs his course through Heaven.
The Moon is less bright.
She borrows her light from the Sun
But keeps her distance until night.
Then the Stars appear like glitter across the sky.
And evening and morning came, the fourth day.

God the Father (within Raphael's story):

Let the waters bring forth living reptiles.
Let birds fly above the Earth, spreading their wings in the air.

Raphael:

God created great whales and every creeping thing.
The waters generated them by their kind.
God saw that it was good.
He blessed them.

God the Father (within Raphael's story)—to the animals:

Be fruitful and multiply.
Fill the seas and lakes and streams.
Let the birds multiply on the Earth.

Raphael:

Then the streams filled with innumerable fishes,
Their shining scales gliding under the green waves.
They graze on seaweed and frolic in the coral.
Some live in pearly shells under rocks.
Some in jointed armor watch.
The seals swim smoothly, and the dolphins play.
The leviathan wallows clumsily with bulky steps.
It is the largest of the living creatures,
As big as a stretch of land,
Breathing with gills and spouting water from his trunk.
The birds burst forth from their eggs
Rupturing shells in kindly destruction.
Soon they grow feathers and fly in the air.
The eagle and stork build their nests in the cliffs and treetops.
The birds know the seasons
And set forth in airish caravans,
Flying over sea and land together.
When evening comes, the nightingale alone sings.
The rooster calls to wake the morning.
The waters are full of fish.
The air is full of birds.
And there was evening and morning—the fifth day.

God the Father (within Raphael's story):

Let Earth bring forth animals,
Cattle and creeping things and beasts of the earth,
Each after their own kind.

Raphael:

Earth opened her womb
And innumerable living creatures poured forth.
They were perfectly formed and fully grown.
The wild beasts came forth and wandered in the forests in pairs.
They walked in the fields and meadows.
Some were solitary and others pastured in herds and flocks.
The grassland broke open and the lion appeared,
Half in the ground and half out, pawing at the earth to get free.
The lynx, leopard, and tiger sprang forth from the earth like moles.
The stag's antlered head rose like branches from the ground.
The behemoth, largest of the land creatures,
Heaved his enormousness out of the earth.
Flocks of sheep arose, fleecy and bleating.
The hippopotamus and crocodile came forth,
Not sure whether they wanted to go to the water or the land.
Then insects and worms crept out of the ground.
The flies waved their wings.
Cracks in the ground burst forth in brightest color
As serpents wriggled forth,
Spotted with purple and gold, turquoise and green.
Some were tiny, others large and fat, and some had wings.
Ants came forth and joined their tribes.
Then the bees swarmed out.
The rest of the creatures are too numerous to count.
You know them, Adam.
You named them.
You know even the huge, hairy-maned serpent—
He is a friend who comes when you call.

Now the Heavens shone in all their glory.
The Earth rotated, clothed in beauty.
The air, water, and earth were filled with birds, fish, and mammals.
But the masterwork was yet to come.
It would be a creature who was not a brute animal like the others.
This new creature would be set apart by reason.
He would walk upright and govern the others.

He would know himself
And be able to communicate with Heaven.
This new creature would worship with heart and voice and eyes,
Adoring the God who made him.

God the Father (within Raphael's story)—to God the Son:

Let us make man in Our image.
Let him rule over the fish of the sea and the birds of the air,
Over the beasts of the field,
Over the whole Earth and everything in it.

Raphael:

He formed you, Adam.
You were dust of the ground,
And into your nostrils He breathed the breath of life.
In His own image, He created you.
He made you male and gave you a female to complete your race.

God the Father (within Raphael's story)—to Adam and Eve:

Be fruitful and multiply. Fill the Earth.
Subdue it and rule over it.

Raphael:

Then He brought you into this delicious garden.
The trees freely provide fruit for you.
Their variety is without end.
But of the Tree of the Knowledge of Good and Evil
You must not eat.
For on the day you eat from it, you will die.
Be careful so sin doesn't surprise you.

God finished creation here.
He looked and saw that it was good.
And there was evening and there was morning—the sixth day.

God stopped working.
He went to the highest Heaven
And looked down on the newly created world.
He saw how good and fair it was.
The Earth and air, the Heavens and constellations
Rang with the song of the ages.

**The Song of the Earth and Air, Heavens and Constellations
(within Raphael's story)**:

Open, everlasting gates!
Open your doors, Heaven!
Let your Creator in.
He has returned from His work.
He has made a world in six days.

Open the gates,
And after this, open them often.
For God will want to visit man often,
And He will send angels with messages frequently,
Messages of grace.

Raphael:

A broad road led from the gates of Heaven
To God's eternal house.
The dust of the road is gold
And the pavement is Stars.
The seventh evening came.
The Sun had set.

The Son arrived at the throne of God
And sat down with His Father.
For He was the One who went to Earth and ordained the work.
He is the author and end of all things.
He rested and blessed the seventh day and made it holy.

The Song of the Heavenly Choirs (within Raphael's story):

Great are Your works, Jehovah.
Infinite is Your power.
No thoughts can measure You.
No tongue can fully tell Your story.
You are greater now than You were before.
You have defeated the rebel spirits.
They thought they could make You less,
But they only succeeded in making You seem greater.
You have turned their evil intentions into a greater good.
You have created man in Your image,
To live on Earth and worship You,
And bring forth each new generation of worshippers.
Their happiness will be multiplied if they continue in righteousness.

Raphael:

Now, I think I have answered your questions
About the creation of the world.
I have told you what happened before you can remember.
You will tell your descendants so they, too, can know.
If there is anything else you want, just ask.

BOOK 8

Narrator:

The angel stopped talking,
But Adam was so entranced that it took him a while to realize it.
Finally, Adam spoke.

Adam:

I can't thank you enough for satisfying my thirst for knowledge.
I would never have known these things without you.
I praise God for the things you have revealed to me.
I have more questions, though,
And only you can answer them.

When I look at the universe, Heaven and Earth,
I can see that compared to everything else
The Earth is just a speck. A grain. An atom.
The Stars inhabit spaces too large to fathom,
But their only purpose is to bring light to Earth.
I don't understand how Nature, whose ways usually make sense,
Could create a universe that is so unbalanced.
Earth should be the servant of the Stars and the Planets,
Not the other way around.

Narrator:

Eve heard Adam speaking these studious thoughts.
She got up and went into the garden.
She didn't want to hear the things the angel was going to say.
Such thoughts were too lofty for her.
She wanted to wait and hear them from Adam instead.

He would tell her more gently,
Mixing in lowly things she could understand
With the more difficult things.
And he would mix them with kisses.
For it wasn't only words she wanted from his lips.
Then Raphael answered Adam.

Raphael:

I don't blame you for asking.
Heaven is God's book for you,
To teach you about His wonderful works.
From the Heavens you learn seasons, hours, days, months, and years.
It doesn't matter whether it is Heaven moving or whether it is Earth.
God doesn't want to be examined.
He wants to be admired.
If anyone tries to understand the Heavens,
God just laughs at their childishness.
When your descendants come to speak of such things,
Of the movements of the spheres, of calculations of the Stars,
God leaves them to their little arguments.

The thing you must consider is this:
Size and brightness are not the same thing as greatness.
The Earth may be small and dull,
But it may contain more good than the Sun.
The Sun shines brightly, but it has no life on it.
It doesn't do any good to itself, only to Earth.
God made the universe enormous
So men would know they were small.
God may use the vastness of space for other things,
But that is not for us to know.
When you see the infinite number of Stars
And the swiftness of the Planets,
You ought to consider the power of God,
Not the mechanisms behind it all.
God is loftier than you can understand.
If you try, you will fail.

What if the Sun is the center of the universe?
What if the Planets dance around the Sun?
You can see them moving, six of them.
What if Earth is a seventh Planet?
What if the Earth itself moves?
The motion of the Planets does not need you to believe in it.
What if the Earth looks like a Planet?
What if it lights up the Moon just like the Moon lights the Earth?
Maybe there is land on the Moon.
The dark spots you see could be clouds.
Clouds make rain, and rain makes plants for food.
The Moon could have inhabitants.
There may be other suns and other moons,
Making light and life possible.
For now, we can only catch a glimpse of their light,
Just as they can only catch a glimpse of ours.
We can argue about it.
We can argue about whether the Sun rises or whether the Earth does.
Does the Sun rise in the East?
Does the Earth begin her journey in the West?
Don't bother your mind about these things.
Leave these things to God.
Serve God and fear Him.
Let Him take care of other worlds,
Wherever they may be.
Take joy in what you have: this Paradise and the beautiful Eve.
Heaven is too high for you to know what happens there.
Be wise.
Think about things that concern you.
Don't dream of other worlds.
Don't wonder about the creatures that live there.
Be content with the revelation you've been given.

Adam:

Oh Raphael! You are pure intelligence.
You have given me both knowledge and simplicity.
I have no more need for anxiety.

It is only when we wander in our thoughts that we are disturbed.
Although it's true that we are apt to wander.
There is no end to our imaginations.
We won't stop until someone warns us,
Or we learn from experience
That it's best to leave such knowledge alone.
We ought to concentrate on our daily tasks.
This is wisdom.
Everything else is just a mental game.
Everything else takes us away from what is important.

Let's stop talking of lofty things.
Let's speak about useful things.
You have told me what happened before I existed.
Now listen to me tell my story.
The day is not over.
Stay with me.

Raphael:

I see that you are graceful and eloquent.
You are made in the image of God,
Whether you talk or not.
We don't think less of you than we do of each other.
We gladly want to learn how God has been dealing with you.
Tell me your story.
I was away that day, guarding the gates of Hell
To make sure not a single one escaped.
We didn't want God's work of creation to be interrupted.
They dare not leave Hell unless God permits it.
The gates of Hell were shut and barricaded.
And from within we heard a lamenting, full of torment and rage.
We were glad when the day was done,
And we could return to Heaven.
But tell me your story now.
I am happily listening.

Adam:

It is hard to tell the story of how human life began.
No one can know his own beginning.
But I will try.
I woke, like someone waking from a deep sleep.
I was lying on soft flowery herbs,
Covered with dewdrops until the Sun dried them.
I turned my eyes toward Heaven.
I saw hills and valleys around me—
Shady woods, sunny plains,
And liquid, murmuring streams.
I saw creatures living, moving, walking, flying.
Birds were singing in the branches.
My heart overflowed with joy.
Then I looked at myself.
I examined my limbs.
I ran back and forth just because I could.
I didn't know where I'd come from.
I didn't know why I existed.
I tried to speak and found that I could.
I named everything I saw:
Sun,
Light,
Earth,
Hills,
Valleys,
Woods,
Plains.
Then I saw the creatures.

Adam (speaking within his own story):

Tell me, creatures, if you saw.
Tell me how I came here.
I didn't do it myself.
Someone made me.
Tell me who it was so I can adore him.

Adam:

While I was calling out, I wandered into the open
And saw the Sun for the first time.
I sat down in a shady, flowered spot and fell asleep.
I thought I was being unmade.
I thought I was being dissolved.
But in my dream, I saw that I was still alive.
Someone came to me in a divine shape.

The Divine Personage (within Adam's story):

Come, Adam. Arise, first man.
You are the first of a numberless race.
You are the first Father.
I will take you to the garden.
Your seat is ready for you.

Adam:

The spirit took me by the hand, and we flew.
It led me up a woody mountain to a plain at the top.
It was an open place, with trees all around.
Everything beautiful I'd seen before
Then seemed plain to me compared to this.
Each tree was full of the most beautiful fruit.
Suddenly I was hungry. I wanted to eat the fruit.
Then I woke up and found that all I'd dreamed was real.
My guide appeared, the one from the dream.
I fell at his feet, rejoicing.
He raised me up.

The Divine Personage (within Adam's story):

I am the One you were looking for.
Everything above you and below you and beneath you
Is yours to take care of.
The fruit of the trees belongs to you.

You will always have food, for I give it freely to you.
But do not eat of the Tree of the Knowledge of Good and Evil.
Don't even taste it.
Be aware that the day you eat it
You will have disobeyed My voice.
From that day, your death will be inevitable.
From that day, you will be mortal.
From that day, you will lose this Paradise.
You will trade it for a world of sorrow.

Adam:

He gave me this command sternly.
Even now my ears are ringing with it,
And I feel afraid.
His face softened and he spoke again.

The Divine Personage (within Adam's story):

Not only is this mountaintop yours,
But the whole Earth.
You will rule over it.
You will rule over all the creatures that live on it.
As a sign of this, I will bring each bird and beast to you.
You will give them their names
And they will swear their loyalty to you.

Adam:

As He spoke, each bird and beast came to me,
Two by two,
Bowing submissively.
God gave my mind knowledge of what they were like.
But in all that I saw, I found something was missing.
There was something I still wanted
And I dared to speak to God about it.

Adam (speaking within his own story):

You are higher than mankind.
I adore You.
You are the maker of the universe.
You have given me every good thing.
But I see that the beasts come two by two,
While I am alone.
Who shall be with me to enjoy this Paradise?
How can I be happy if I am alone?

Adam:

I was presumptuous to speak,
But God answered me.

God the Father (within Adam's story):

Of course you are not alone.
The Earth is full of creatures.
The air is full of birds.
All you have to do is ask
And any one of them will come and play before you.
You know their language and their ways.
You can pass the time with them.
You are their ruler

Adam (speaking within his own story):

Please don't be offended, Oh my Maker.
But You have made me like You.
These other creatures are inferior to me,
Just as I am inferior to You.
What delight can I find in those who are less than me?
Harmony must be mutual.
There must be give and take.
With these there will be an imbalance.
We will be tiresome to each other.

I am looking for fellowship.
I want to be with another rational creature.
An animal will not satisfy my need.
Birds don't converse with animals.
Fish don't converse with birds.
Oxen don't converse with apes.
There is an even bigger chasm between men and beasts
Than there is between beasts of one kind and beasts of another.

God the Father (within Adam's story):

You seek happiness with a companion, Adam?
What do you think of Me, then?
I am as I am.
Do you think I am happy?
There is no one like Me.
I have no equal.
I have no one to talk to but my creatures,
And they are all inferior to Me,
Much more inferior than the animals are to you.

Adam, humbly (speaking within his own story):

You are perfect and complete in Yourself.
I am not like that.
I need another to make me complete.
You don't need to have children.
You are already infinite.
You are One and yet have an infinite number of parts.
But a man, as one, is merely alone.
He must have children to multiply his image,
And this requires love and companionship.
You keep yourself company,
Or if you like, you raise one of your creatures up to your level.
I can't do that with the animals.
I can't raise them to my level.

God the Father (within Adam's story)—unoffended:

It pleases Me that you can see the difference
Between yourself and an animal.
You have been made in My image.
The animals were not.
I have always known it is not good for you to be alone.
I paraded the animals before you so you would know it, too.
What I am going to make next will make you happy:
A helper, made like you—
Your other self—
Your heart's desire.

Adam:

When He stopped speaking, I was overwhelmed.
I sank down, dazzled and exhausted, and I slept.
But as I slept, I dreamed.
In my dream I saw the shape of God,
Stooping by my left side,
Removing one of my ribs.
My bodily fluids rushed out, blood and lymph.
Then, just as quickly, my wounds knit themselves back together.
God made a creature from my rib,
A creature like a man,
But a different sex.
Every beautiful thing I'd ever seen
Now seemed ugly compared to her.
I woke, hoping to find her.
She was my only hope of happiness now.
Then I saw her, just as she was in my dream.
She had every good thing that Heaven could give a person.
God led her to me, although I couldn't see Him.
She knew about marriage and what it meant.
Grace was in her steps.
Heaven was in her eyes.
Her every gesture was full of dignity and love.
I was overwhelmed.

Adam (speaking within his own story):

This is what I wanted!
You have done as You promised, my benevolent Creator!
This is the best of all Your gifts.
She is bone of my bone,
Flesh of my flesh.
She shall be called Woman because she came out of Man.
For this reason, a man shall leave his father and mother
And cling to his wife.
They shall be one flesh, one heart, one soul.

Adam:

The woman heard me.
She was mine, yet she was innocent and virginal.
Her modesty and her knowledge of her own worth
Would not permit her to come to me without being wooed.
She was shy and pure.
When she saw me, she turned away
And I followed her.
I led her to our bridal bed.
The Heavens and the Stars gave their best influence.
The nightingale sang a wedding song.
The wind whispered happily in the woods.
This was bliss itself.
Here I felt her touch and first knew passion.

I felt weak.
Maybe what was taken from my side was too much for me to lose,
For she was everything.
I understood that her mind was inferior to mine.
I saw that she was less like God than I.
She didn't have a desire to dominate other creatures.
But she was complete in herself.
Whatever she said was the wisest,
The most virtuous,
The most appropriate,

And the best thing.
Everything in my mind went away when I looked at her.
My wisdom turned to foolishness when I spoke to her.
I was in awe of her, as though she were far better than I.

An Angelic Voice within Adam's story:

You are not less than she.
Be wise.
Do your part.
She will not desert you.
She is not better than you.
You are overcome by her beauty,
By the external.
She is beautiful and worthy to be cherished,
And honored,
And loved.
But you are not to be ruled by her.
You are worthy.
The more you know your own value,
The more she will acknowledge you as her leader.

She was made beautiful to bring you delight.
If you think that sexual pleasure is the best thing there is,
Think again.
Don't the animals also mate?
There is nothing about mating to bring delight to you.
Love her for her mind, her beauty, and her humanity.
Love these things about her.
Love her with your mind.
That is the kind of love that will enlarge your heart and mind.

It's not a heavenly love,
Nor is it the mating of beasts.
If that was all you wanted,
You would have been satisfied with an animal.

Adam, embarrassed (speaking within his own story):

It's not her outward beauty,
Or the pleasure of mating like animals that brings me joy.
I love everything about her.
I love the thousand little things she says and does every day.
I love her sweetness, her compliance, her love.
These are the things that bring us unity.
This is deeper than lust.
I love her with a heavenly love.

But I want to know . . .
Do heavenly spirits love like this?
How do they show love?
Just by looking at one another?
Or do they mix their spirits in some sort of virtual touching?

The Angel (within Adam's story)—smiling indulgently:

It's enough for you to know we are happy.
Whatever purity of love you enjoy,
We enjoy also, but in spirit instead of in body.
We can embrace, air meeting air,
Spirit meeting spirit,
Purity meeting purity.
We don't need bodies to bring us together.
But the Sun is setting.
It is time that I left.
Be strong.
Live happily.
Love.

And remember—to love God is to obey Him.
You must keep His great command.
Blessings or curses for all generations are in your hands.
Stand fast.
This task is left to your free will.
You can stand against temptation.

Narrator:

Then Raphael rose and Adam bade him farewell.

Adam:

Go to God, my heavenly guest.
I am grateful that you took time to treat me as a friend.
Show kindness to us and return often.

Narrator:

The angel went up to Heaven,
And Adam went to his bed.

BOOK 9 PART 1 REFERENCES

Achilles *(man):* Hero of Homer's *Iliad*, dies in the Trojan War

Aeneas *(man):* Hero of Virgil's *Aeneid*, founds a new settlement for the displaced Trojans after the Trojan War

Hera *(goddess):* Wife of Zeus and queen of the Greek gods, known for her jealousy

Homer *(man):* Ancient Greek who wrote the *Iliad* and the *Odyssey*

Lavinia *(woman):* In Virgil's *Aeneid*, Lavinia is the princess Aeneas marries.

Tigris River *(place):* The book describes the Tigris River as springing forth from Eden, going underground, and coming up as a fountain by the Tree of Life. Historically, the Tigris River is one of the boundaries of Mesopotamia (the other being the Euphrates River). It flows through the current countries of Turkey, Iraq, and Syria.

Turnus *(man):* In Virgil's *Aeneid*, Turnus was betrothed to Lavinia, but she was destined to marry Aeneas.

BOOK 9: PART 1

Satan plans his attack, and Adam and Eve debate
whether they should separate for the day's work

Milton:

I will not talk anymore
About God and angels
Sitting and eating with men like friends.

I must now tell a tragic tale,
A tale of disloyalty, revolt, and disobedience.
God has become distant and disgusted.
He is angry.
His judgment is just,
Even though it brought so much sadness to the world.
For sin and misery came to mankind,
And they foreshadowed death.

It is a sad task
But no sadder than
Homer's story of Achilles
Or Turnus striving for the hand of Lavinia,
Or Hera's rage against Aeneas.

My own heavenly muse
Who visits me by night
And dictates to me as I dream—
Or inspires my poetry—
Shall give me the words to say.

It took a long time for me to decide to write my epic.
I don't want to talk of wars,
Which until now have been the only venue for writing about heroics.

I don't want to write long, tedious stories about knights and battles
And how they became long-suffering and heroic martyrs.
I don't want to describe races and games,
Jousts or lances or shields,
Horses and their glittering coverings.
I don't want to talk about feasts in banquet halls.
It doesn't matter how skilled I am
Or what my position is.
That's not what makes a poem heroic.

I am not skilled or studious.
I write for a higher purpose.
I am growing old and tired.
I need the Muse to bring the words to my mind.

Narrator:

The Sun has gone down.
Twilight has ended.
Darkness has come.
It was then that Satan came.
He had just fled from Gabriel's threats.
Now, full of fraud and malice,
And even more intent on destroying mankind,
And unconcerned about his own fate,
At midnight he returned.

He was afraid of day
Since the Sun saw him coming
And warned the angels who were guarding the Earth.
For seven nights he traveled only in darkness,
Staying on the dark side of the Earth.
On the eighth night, he returned
On the opposite side from the entrance
Where the cherubim were watching.
Stealthy, he sneaked in.

In these early days,
The Tigris River sprang forth from Eden
And went underground.
It emerged as a fountain by the Tree of Life.
Satan swam in the river and rose in the fountain.
He looked like the mist.
Then he looked for a place to hide.
He had already searched all the land
From Eden to the Black Sea,
From the Sea of Azof,
Beyond the shores of Siberia.
He went as far south as the Antarctic.
He went as far west as Syria and all the way to the Ocean.
He explored the isthmus of Panama
All the way to India and the Ganges River.
He roamed the globe, searching.
He considered every creature
To find out which would work best for him.

The serpent, he decided, would be the best.
The serpent was subtle and stealthy.
He could enter into it and hide.
No one would suspect evil to come from a snake.
Snakes are clever and witty.
They are naturally thoughtful.
If anyone saw another animal acting like a demon
They would be suspicious.
But the natural intellect of the snake
Would be the best disguise for him.
His decision was made,
But first, he poured out his grief in a passionate complaint.

Satan:

Oh Earth! You are so much like Heaven!
God has made you good.
It makes sense.
Why would he make something that wasn't?

The Earth's sky is surrounded by the Heavens.
The Heavens shine with the lights of the Sun, Moon, and Stars.
Those lights shine their beams onto the Earth,
Bringing their precious influence to it.

Earth is at the center,
Receiving blessings from all the other worlds.
The other worlds get nothing in return.
They exist to bless the Earth.
The Earth produces plants and herbs
And other creatures that grow, sense, and reason,
And man is the highest of all the creatures.

I could have had great delight in you, Oh Earth,
If I could have lived in the hills and valleys,
Rivers, woods, and plains,
Land, seas, and shores covered with forests,
Rocks, dens, and caves.
But I can't find refuge in any of these.
The more pleasures I see
The more I am tormented.
It is a study in opposites.
All that is good, to me seems to be evil.
In Heaven itself, it would be much worse,
For there is even greater good there,
And so to me, greater evil.

But I don't want to live here on Earth,
Nor do I want to live in Heaven—
Unless I am the ruler there.
I am not even trying to make myself less miserable.
I just want to cause misery to others.

Even though destroying will make things worse for me,
It is only when I destroy that my tortured mind can rest.

I will destroy him,
Or win him over so that he longs for his own destruction.

It will happen.
He will choose evil and woe.

Destruction shall cover the Earth,
And I will be the most glorious of the hellish powers.
For in one day, I will deface
What it took God six days to make.

And who knows how long it took Him to think of it?
Maybe He only started thinking of it
When I freed a third of the angels
From humiliating servitude to Him.
To avenge the loss of His angels,
He made a creature out of the dirt
And gave him the image of Himself.

That image should have belonged to us!
He said it.
He did it.
He made man
He made this whole world for him.
He crowned man the ruler of this world.

He made the angels the servants of men.
It's so humiliating!
Angels must watch and tend these creatures.

I don't want the angelic guardians to stop me.
I must wrap myself in mist
And glide stealthily through every bush
So I can find the serpent sleeping.
I will hide myself and my evil intentions
Neatly in his winding folds.
Oh what a fall!
I used to be with God in the highest place.
Now I must enmesh myself with a slimy beast.
I wanted to be a god,
But now I must inhabit a brute.

But because I am ambitious,
And because I want revenge,
I must do it
Whoever wants something
Must pay the price,
Going as low down as he was high up before.
Revenge is sweet at first,
But it is bitter in the end.

I don't care.
I want to destroy this new favorite of Heaven.
He is a man made of clay.
God made him out of dust just to spite us.
And we will pay him back in spite.

Narrator:

He said this as he crept through the bushes
Like a black mist at midnight,
Looking to find the serpent.
He found him curled into a labyrinth
With his head tucked in the middle.
And his head was full of crafty plans.
He wasn't hiding like snakes now do,
Waiting to pounce on their prey.
Snakes were not harmful yet.

The serpent slept on the grass without fear.
The Devil entered his mouth
And possessed his mind and heart,
Filling them with intelligence.

But the serpent did not wake.
He was waiting for the morning.

When the light began to dawn in Eden
And the flowers gave off their dewy scents,
Breathing praise to their Creator,

The humans smelled the aroma
And came out to join the choir in its worship of God.
They spoke of how they might best do their work that day.
The garden had grown wide because of their work
And it was hard for two to do the job.
And Eve spoke to her husband.

Eve:

Adam, we have much work to do in this garden.
It is pleasant to tend the plants and herbs and flowers.
But until more people come to join in the work,
It is impossible to keep up with it.
Whatever we prune in the day
Grows back in the night.
The garden is becoming wild.
Now listen to my idea.
Let's divide the work.
You can go where you want,
Or where the work is most needed,
Whether to bind the vines to the arbor,
Or to direct the ivy where to climb.
I will work in the rose garden.
If we work too closely together,
We will find ourselves looking at each other,
And smiling and talking,
Which will interrupt our work.
We won't finish anything,
Even if we start early and don't finish until suppertime.

Adam:

My only Eve,
I love you more than anything.
This is a good idea.
You are thinking clearly about how to do our work.
I praise you for your foresight.
For nothing is more beautiful

Than for a woman to study the household tasks
And encourage her husband in good works.

But God hasn't called us to work so hard
That we can't stop for food or conversation.
Conversation is food for the mind.
Smiles bring reason to our minds,
Lifting us higher than the animals.
Smiles are the food of love,
And love is a lofty goal.

God didn't call us to unending work,
But to delight joined with reason.

We will be able to keep our garden
From growing back into the wilderness
Until younger hands come to help us.

I guess I could agree to a short separation of tasks.
Sometimes solitude is welcome.
And a short break from each other
Will only make us long for each other more.

But I have another problem with this.
I don't want harm to come to you while you're not with me.
You know we were warned.
An enemy is envious of our happiness.
In his despair, he will try to attack us,
To bring us to shame and woe.
He is watching us, no doubt,
Hoping to find the best time for his attack.
If we are not together
We will not be able to help each other.

He might try to make us disloyal to God.
He might try to disturb our love for each other.
It is safest for a wife to remain close to her husband
When she knows that danger and dishonor lurk close by.

Her husband will guard her,
Or endure the attack with her.

Eve, annoyed, but ever sweet:

Oh offspring of Heaven and Earth,
And Ruler of the Earth,
I know we have an enemy who wants to ruin us.
But I didn't expect you to doubt my loyalty
Just because we have an enemy.
Don't be afraid of his violence.
For we do not have either pain or death.
He is tricking you into doubting me.
Can my love be shaken by his fraud?
How can you think such things of me, Adam?

Adam, trying to calm Eve:

Oh Daughter of God, immortal Eve,
You are free from sin and blame.
It's not because I doubt you
That I don't want you out of my sight.
I'm trying to avoid an attack altogether.
Even though I know he won't succeed in tempting us,
It's an insult that he would even try.
It means he thinks we are corruptible
And able to be tempted.
Then we would become angry.
That's what I'm trying to avoid.

If we're together, the enemy won't attack.
I'm sure if we were separated
He would attack me first.
He must be a clever enemy
If he was able to seduce angels to join him.
It also shows that he is not above asking for help.

When you are with me, I have every virtue.
When you see me, I am wiser,
More watchful,
Stronger.
If I felt shame while you were watching,
I would fight against it with all my power.
Don't you feel the same way about me?
Wouldn't you rather face the enemy with me?

Narrator:

Adam answered her in a loving fashion,
But Eve thought he still doubted her.
She replied again in the sweetest tones.

Eve:

If this is what it comes down to,
That we're changing what we do
Because we are afraid of the enemy,
How can we still call ourselves free and happy?
He can harm us,
But he can't make us sin.
We will be offended because he thinks we are weak,
But that is not our fault.
That evil is just in his own foul mind.
So why should we be afraid of him?
We'll have twice as much honor
Once we prove he's wrong.
We'll have peace within
And favor from Heaven
Once they see how we handle the attack.

For what good are faith, love, and virtue
Unless they are tested and proved true?
Let's not assume that our happy state is so incomplete.
God is wise.
Our happiness is not worth much

If it doesn't endure whether we are together or alone.
And if this is so, then our Paradise is no Paradise after all.

Adam, fervently:

Oh Woman,
God's will is what's best.
His hand of creation didn't leave anything imperfect or deficient
In any part of His creation
And especially in us.
Anything that might make us secure
He has within Himself.
It is all within His power.
Nothing can cause us harm unless He permits it.

But God left us free will.
He created reason as a good thing,
But He told us to be watchful and alert
So that something that looked good to the mind
Might lead us to reason incorrectly
And lead our will
So that we do the thing that God has forbidden.

I'm not nagging because I don't trust you.
I am reminding you of this because I love you.
And I want you to remind me also.

We stand firm,
But the possibility of swerving is there.
We may be deceived without knowing it
If we don't keep watch.

Don't go looking for temptation.
It's better to avoid it and stay with me.
The trial will come even if we don't go looking for it.
If I'm with you, I can testify that you obeyed God.
But if you think it's safer to pretend the enemy doesn't exist,
Then go.

For if you stay when you don't want to
Then you are farther from me than if you just went off alone.
Go and rely on your natural innocence and your virtue.
God has given you all you need.
It remains only for you to do your part.

Narrator:

So the Patriarch of Mankind spoke.
Eve persisted, but in a more submissive manner.

Eve:

With your permission then,
And having been warned
That our trial will come when we're not looking for it,
I will go willingly.
I don't think such a proud enemy
Will attack the weaker one of us first.
He'd be ashamed to do it.

Narrator:

She pulled her hand out of Adam's hand
And slipped off through the woods,
As softly as a wood-nymph or a goddess.

Adam watched her go.
He was delighted in her,
But he would have been happier if she'd stayed.

He repeated his words to her,
To return to him by noon
So they might share the noontime meal
And an afternoon rest.

Oh much deceived, much failing, unsuspecting Eve!
Oh perverse event!

For you will never return from your last hour in Paradise.
You won't find a sweet feast or a sound nap.
For the enemy is waiting in the flowers and shadows
To ambush you with hellish malice.
He is waiting to steal your innocence and faith and bliss.

For now, since the sunrise,
The devil, disguised as a serpent,
Came forth to find the two humans,
Who were every person in the whole race.

BOOK 9 PART 2 REFERENCES

Athens *(place):* Athens was the heart of ancient Greece, the place where democracy was founded.

Delilah *(woman):* In the Bible, Delilah was Samson's lover. She betrayed him to the Philistines, bringing about his downfall.

Rome *(place):* Rome was the capital of the ancient Roman Empire.

Samson *(man):* In the Bible, Samson is a judge (leader) of Israel. He was known for his superhuman strength and for his weakness for woman.

Solomon *(man):* In the Bible, Solomon is the son of King David and ruled after him, building a lavish temple for God.

BOOK 9: PART 2

Satan successfully tempts Eve,
who then draws Adam into her sin.

Narrator:

Satan sought his prey in shady spots and fields.
He looked in all the groves and pleasant gardens.
By fountains and streams he looked for them.
What he really wanted was to find Eve alone.
But that hardly ever happened.

When he saw Eve alone in the rose garden,
It was beyond his wildest hopes.
She was working in the flowers,
Red, purple, blue, or speckled with gold,
Tying them gently so that they could stand.
She didn't know that she was one of them,
That she was a fair, unsupported flower,
And that the storm was near.

He came closer,
Hiding among the trees of cedar, pine, and palm.
In and out he wove,
Watching Eve's hand as it worked among the flowers.
It was more beautiful than the gardens of Adonis,
Even more beautiful than the garden
Where Solomon took his Egyptian wife.

He admired the garden, but he admired the woman more.
Like a person who has been cooped up
In a filthy, stinking, crowded city,
Delights when he comes into the country
Among farms and fresh, country scents,

The devil took delight in Eden.
And he took even more delight when he saw Eve.
Her graceful innocence,
And her every gesture
Seemed to overcome his malice
And took the fierceness out of his attack.

For a second, the evil one stepped outside of himself
And set aside his hatred, envy, and revenge.
For a second, he was good.

But the hot Hell inside him always burns.
Soon the burning returned to torture him even more.
For he knew the pleasures were not for him.
Then he remembered his hatred,
And his thoughts of evildoing.

Satan:

Where have my sweet thoughts led me?
I've been so entranced by the beauty of the garden
That I've forgotten what brought me here!
I didn't come to love, but to hate.
I didn't come to turn Hell into Paradise,
But to destroy the pleasures they have,
For destruction is my only joy.
All other pleasures are lost to me.

I can't pass up this opportunity.
The woman is alone,
Waiting to be attacked.
Her husband is not near,
For I have looked for him.
I don't want to attack him.
He is more intellectual than this one,
And stronger
And built like a hero, although an earthly one.
I have no hope of wounding him.

I, myself, have been wounded.
Hell has brought me so low
And pain made me so weak
Compared to what I was when I was in Heaven.

She is divinely beautiful,
Fit for the gods to love.
Beauty is the way to ruin her.
I will deceive her with a show of love.

Narrator:

Satan, the enemy of mankind, spoke these words
While he was in the form of a serpent.
He made his way toward Eve,
Not slithering on the ground
As serpents do today.
He coiled his long body in a circle,
With his head on top,
And bounced on the coils.
His eyes were like jewels
And his neck like greenish gold.
His shape was pleasing and lovely.
There has never been a more beautiful snake,
not even those from ancient legends.

The snake approached obliquely at first,
Like one who wanted to come close but feared to interrupt.
He sidled along
Like a ship navigating the river's mouth,
Or the shore when the wind is violent.
Like a sailor who shifts the sails to account for the wind,
The snake varied his path.
He curled many times where Eve could see him
He wanted her to admire him.

She was busy.
She heard the sound of rustling leaves,

But she didn't pay attention to it.
She was used to noises in the field.
For all the beasts would come when she called them.

The snake grew bolder now.
He uncoiled before her and stood.
He looked at her with admiration.
He bowed to her repeatedly
And licked the ground where she had stepped.
Finally, she turned to look at him.
His gentle, dumb expression caught her eye.
He was glad to have her attention at last.
Using the serpent's tongue and the air around it,
He began his temptation of Eve.

Satan:

Don't be surprised if I stare at you.
I should fear you, for you are a wonder.
You look like your Maker.
Every living creature loves to look at you.
Everything adores you for your beauty.
But here in this wild garden,
Do you only have these crude, lowly animals to admire you?
Is there only one man who understands the depth of your beauty?
One is not very many.
You should be a goddess among the gods,
Adored and served by angels who follow you like servants.

Narrator:

The tempter oozed compliments
And tuned the prelude to his attack.
His words made their way into Eve's heart,
Though she marveled at his voice.
In amazement, she finally spoke.

Eve:

What does this mean?
Have I really heard an animal speak like a man?
Can an animal think?
I thought no animal could speak.
God, when He created them, did not give them that ability.
Perhaps the animals can think.
I see something of that in their eyes and their actions.
I have seen you before, serpent.
But I didn't know you could speak.
Tell me how this miracle occurred.
How is it that you acquired the power of speech?
And why are you so friendly to me
And so much higher than the other beasts?
Tell me, for I long to know.

Satan:

Oh Empress of this lovely world,
Beautiful Eve . . .
It is easy for me to tell you everything you want to know.
Your wish is my command.
At first, I was like the other animals.
My thoughts were lowly.
All I could understand was food and mating.
I couldn't ponder anything loftier than those.
But one day I saw a tree in the distance.
It was full of fruits of various colors, red and gold.
I went closer so I could see it more clearly,
And a breeze blew through the tree,
Bringing savory odors to my senses.
It was sweeter than fennel
Or than the new milk of a ewe at twilight.
I had a sharp desire to taste those apples.
I resolved to do so at once,
For hunger and thirst are powerful persuaders.
Stirred up by the sweet scent,

I moved toward the tree.
I wound myself around the mossy trunk.
The other beasts watched.
They, too, wanted the fruit,
But it was too high for them to reach.
I slithered up the tree to the fruit and ate my fill.
I had never had such pleasure before.
At long last, my appetite was satisfied.
But before long, I knew there had been a change in me.
I had the power of reason and speech,
Even though I remained in body a serpent.

I turned my thoughts to things that were high and deep
And considered everything I saw
In Heaven, in Earth, and in-between.
Everything I saw was beautiful and good.
But in you I saw the beauty of the divine.
Nothing could compare to your loveliness.
That is what made me come to you,
To gaze upon your loveliness
And worship you,
Queen of the creatures and universal Woman.

Eve, amazed, but not worried:

Serpent, you are praising me too much.
It makes me think the fruit you ate
Has not done you as much good as you think it has.

But where is this tree?
How far is it from here?
For there are many trees in Paradise,
And there are many we have not yet discovered.
The abundance that was given to us
Means that a great amount of fruit has never been touched.

Satan, with wicked glee:

Empress, I will show you the way.
It is not far—
Beyond a row of myrtles in a flat place by a fountain,
Just past a thicket of myrrh and balm.
If you let me, I will take you there.

Eve:

Lead me, then.

Narrator:

The snake rolled and tangled himself as he led her.
Hope made him happy,
And joy made all his colors brighter,
As though he were lit by a flame.
But it was like an evil flame,
An oily vapor of the night,
Which people often say is a sign of evil spirits,
Hovering and blazing and intending to deceive.
These flames often lead night-wanderers
Into bogs and mires,
Through ponds or pools,
To be swallowed up and lost.

The wily snake led Eve to the Tree,
To the very Tree that had been forbidden to her,
The Tree of all our woe.

Eve:

Serpent, you have led me uselessly.
Although this tree is full of fruit,
It is fruitless to me.
Obviously, the fruit has caused a wondrous miracle in you.
But we have been forbidden to taste or touch this fruit.

God gave us His command.
It was His only restriction on us.
Everything else is ours to command as we see fit.

Satan, slickly:

Really?
Has God said that you can't eat the fruit of any of these trees?
How can that be when He has declared you lords of the Earth?

Eve:

We can eat the fruit of any of the trees in the garden.
But we may not eat the fruit of this particular tree.
For God has said "You shall not eat of it,
Nor shall you touch it,
Or you will die."

Narrator:

When she had scarcely finished talking,
The tempter addressed her more boldly.
He pretended to show love toward mankind.
He pretended to be angry at the wrong God had done to mankind.
The snake moved passionately,
Yet beautifully,
As though he were one of the great orators of old.
He was like one in Athens or Rome,
Where eloquence flourished,
Though it has since died.
He spoke like he was defending a great cause,
Using every gesture to win his audience even before he spoke.
Then he spoke most passionately.

Satan:

Oh sacred, wise, and wisdom-giving plant,
Mother of knowledge,

Now I feel your power within me.
I understand cause and effect.
I understand the ways of the angels of the highest ranks.

Queen of the Universe,
Don't believe God's rigid threats of death.
You shall not die.
How could that be?
Will the fruit kill you?
The fruit will give you a life of knowledge.
Will God kill you?
Look at me!
I have touched and tasted the fruit,
And I'm still alive.
I'm living a life more complete than the one fate meant for me.
I have ventured higher than my fate.
Shall this higher life be forbidden to Man,
Which is available to beasts?
Will God kill for such a little infraction of His law?
God will praise your courage and virtue
If you look death in the face,
Whatever death is.
He will know that you're brave enough to seek a higher life
And the knowledge of good and evil,
Even in the face of danger.
How could it be wrong to know what is good?
And if evil is real,
Then knowing about it can only help you avoid it.
God cannot punish you and call it justice.
And we know that God is just.
So don't be afraid.
You don't need to obey.
Because you fear death, you are safe.

Why was this forbidden to you?
It was to keep you low and ignorant.
It was to keep you in awe of God.
God knows that in the day that you eat this fruit

Your dim eyes will become open and clear.
You will be like gods,
Knowing good and evil, just like they do.
If the fruit could make a snake as rational as a man,
What will it do to a man like you?
You'll also become higher than you are.
You'll become a god.
Maybe that's what He meant by death.
It will be a little like death,
Because you won't be human anymore.
You'll leave that behind when you become a god.
This is a death you should want.

Why shouldn't you want to become a god?
Eat their food.
Become one of them.
They are our rulers.
They use their power to make us believe everything they say.
I question that.
They say they gave us life.
But from what I understand,
The Earth is warmed by the Sun.
It is the Earth and Sun that give rise to life—
Not the gods.

But even if they did make all things,
Then it was they who shut the knowledge of good and evil in a tree.
Why should they be offended if you want that knowledge too?
How can your knowing hurt God?
If the tree belongs to God,
And He doesn't want you to have knowledge,
How can the tree give it to you against His will?
The answer to this question
And the answers to many more
Will be yours when you eat this fruit.
Oh goddess, reach for the fruit, then, and taste.

Narrator:

The serpent's words wormed their way into her heart.
She gazed longingly at the fruit.
Just looking at it was a temptation in itself,
But on top of that, the serpent's words resounded in her ears.
His words sounded reasonable to her,
And full of truth.
It was nearly noon, and she was hungry,
And she was made even more hungry
By the smell of the savory fruit.
She wanted it.
She longed for it.
But she paused.

Eve's thoughts:

Oh, greatest of fruits,
You are full of virtue.
Yet you are kept from Man.
Eating the fruit gave voice to the voiceless.
It taught a tongue not created for speech to talk
And to speak your praise.
God also praises you,
Naming the tree the Tree of Knowledge—
Knowledge of both good and evil.
But he forbids us to eat your fruit.
His forbidding only makes you greater,
For it tells us that there is something you have which we lack.
It makes us humble,
For we know that there is a good thing that we do not possess.

I see that He has forbidden us to know.
He forbids good to us.
He forbids us to be wise.
A rule like this is not binding.
But if death is the punishment,
If we are then bound by death,

Then what good is it to have a freer mind?
In the day we eat of the fruit, we shall die.

But what about the serpent?
He has eaten and lives.
He knows and speaks and reasons and discerns,
Despite being an irrational beast before.
Was death invented for man alone?
Or is this intellectual food given to beasts alone
And not to man?
I guess it was.
But the beast who ate it doesn't envy us our higher position.
He comes to us joyfully,
To tell us of the good thing that has happened to him.
He is friendly to mankind.
He is not full of lies.
Why should I be afraid?
How can I even know what fear means?
I can't know.
Not while I'm ignorant of good and evil.
Not while I'm ignorant of God and death.
Not while I'm ignorant of law and penalty.
This fruit is the cure for my ignorance.
This divine fruit,
This beautiful fruit,
This delicious fruit
Will bring me wisdom.
What's stopping me from reaching for it
And tasting it
And feeding both my body and my mind?

Narrator:

In that evil hour, her greedy hand reached for the fruit.
She plucked it and ate it.
Earth felt the wound.
All nature sighed with woe.
All was lost.

The serpent slunk back to the thicket. But it didn't matter.
Eve wasn't paying attention to him anymore.
All she could think of was the taste of the fruit.
She had never tasted anything so delightful,
Or so she thought.
It might have been a result of her high expectations.
Greedily, she gorged herself without restraint.
She didn't know she was eating death.
She satisfied her appetite.
She felt drunk.
She was happy and pleased with herself.

Eve:

Oh sovereign, virtuous, and best of all the trees in Paradise!
You have the power to give wisdom!
I thought your fruit was evil,
And created for no purpose.
But from here on out, I will take care of you.
Every morning, I will tend you
And ease the burden of the heavy fruit on your branches.
I will eat your fruit until I grow mature in knowledge.
I will become like the gods who know everything.
For if this fruit had been for the gods,
It would not have grown here in the garden.
You, oh Tree, are my best guide to wisdom.
I was ignorant until I followed you.
You have opened the way to wisdom!
You have given me access to it.
Though it was hidden, it is now hidden in me.

Heaven is high and remote.
Perhaps no one there saw me eat.
Maybe they were distracted by other concerns
And failed to keep watch over the Tree.
But how shall I tell Adam?
Shall I tell him how I've changed?
Should I give him fruit so he can become as happy as I am,

Or should I keep the power of knowledge to myself?
If I keep it to myself, I'll be his equal.
The fruit has made up for the things that made me less than he is.
He will love me more if I am more equal to him,
And even sometimes superior to him.
An inferior person cannot be fully free.

This is a good idea,
But what if God saw me, and death comes?
Then I shall be no more.
God will give Adam another Eve,
And he will live with her and enjoy her.
And I will be dead.

I think it's best, in light of this,
That I share this fruit with Adam,
Whether it brings me happiness or woe.
I love him so much that with him,
I could endure a thousand deaths.
Without him, life is nothing to me.

Narrator:

After she said this, she turned from the tree.
But she had worshipped a thing.
She had worshipped the power within the tree.
For the knowledge-filled sap of the tree
Was made from nectar, the drink of the gods.

Adam, all the while, had been waiting for her to return.
He had woven her a garland of flowers for her hair,
A fitting reward for her morning's work.
Just like reapers adorn their harvest queen,
He promised himself great joy at her return
And great comfort, because he had waited so long.
But deep in his heart he suspected something was wrong.
He felt his confidence falter
And went forth to meet her.

He found her near the Tree.
In her hand she held a branch full of fruit.
The smell wafted over him.
First, she gave her excuses,
And then her defense.

Eve:

Did you wonder what took me so long?
I missed you.
Being away from you felt like forever.
I never mean to be parted from you again for so long.
But the reason I was gone so long is both strange and wonderful.
This Tree is not what we were told.
It's not dangerous to taste.
It doesn't open the way to evil.
Instead, it opens the eyes of the one who eats of it.
It makes them like gods.
The wise serpent,
Who doesn't have the same rules as we do,
Or if he does, he disobeys them,
Ate the fruit.
He didn't die!
From the minute he ate the fruit,
He got a human voice and human reasoning powers.
He argued his case so persuasively
That I also tasted the fruit
And found that he was right.
It opened my eyes, which were dim before.
It broadened my soul.
It deepened my heart.
It made me begin to become a god.
That was a thing I wanted mostly for your sake,
Not for my own.
For whatever makes you happy makes me happy.
If I don't share this growth with you, it's no good!
Taste the fruit!
We can then share this joy,

Just as we share our love.
If you don't taste, we won't be the same anymore.
It will drive a wedge between us.
And even if I try to renounce my godhood,
Fate will not permit it.

Narrator:

Eve told her story with a blithe and happy face,
But there was irritation flushing her cheeks.
On the other side, Adam stood amazed
To hear of the fatal deed Eve had done.
He felt as though he had been turned to stone and his mind erased.
Chills of horror ran through his veins.
He dropped the garland he had made for Eve,
And the petals fell from the roses.
He was speechless and pale for a long time.
Finally, he broke his inward silence
And spoke to himself.

Adam, to himself:

Oh, fairest of all creation,
The best thing I can see or think of,
My holy, divine, good, friendly, and sweet one!
Suddenly you are lost, defaced, deflowered,
And devoted to death.
How can this be?
How did you give in to disobedience?
How could you violate the forbidden fruit?
Some cursed lie of the enemy tricked you, but you can't see it yet.
And at the same time, you have ruined me.
For I must die with you.
How can I live without you?
How can I give up our sweet fellowship and love?
How can I live alone in these wild woods?

If I had another rib to spare
And God made another Eve,
I would still mourn for you.
I would still feel our union drawing me.
You are flesh of my flesh
And bone of my bone.
Whatever happens to you must happen to me too,
Whether it is happiness or woe.

Narrator:

After he thought these things,
His despair turned into submission.
There was no cure.
In this state of calm, he turned to Eve.

Adam:

What a bold thing you have done, my adventuresome Eve.
You have roused great danger.
Even if all you did was covet the sacred fruit,
It would have been bad.
But tasting it is much worse!
Whatever has happened can't be undone.
But maybe you won't die.
Maybe it's not so bad.
Perhaps when the serpent tasted the fruit,
It turned into a regular fruit instead of a holy one.
By the time you ate it, it was okay.
After all, the serpent didn't die.
Like you said, he is alive,
And the life he lives is that of a man,
A life of a higher degree.
I can see why this made you want to try the fruit.
You thought we would be made higher too.
A higher degree of life for us could only mean
That we would be gods, or at least angels.
I don't think that God, our wise Creator,

Will destroy us, the highest of His creations.
He gave us so much,
Putting us in authority over all His works.
When we fall, they must fall too,
Because they were created for us
And are dependent on us.
God could destroy everything and make it all again,
But there's no way He would want to destroy us.
If he did such a thing, the enemy would win.
The enemy would say, "God's favor is fleeting and fickle.
Who can please such a God for long?
First He ruined me and now mankind.
Whom will he ruin next?"
God will not want him to say these things.
But if you are doomed, then I must be doomed with you.
If death comes to you,
Then death is life to me.
This is how strong our bond is.
Whatever you are is mine.
We cannot be separated.
We are one.
If I lose you, then I lose myself.

Eve:

What a glorious expression of love!
What a glowing example!
I love you also but fall short of your perfection.
Adam, I sprang forth from your side,
And I am glad to hear you talk of our unbreakable union—
One heart,
One soul.
Your declaration is proof of it.
Death—or anything worse than death—shall not separate us.
We are linked by love.
You will participate with me in one guilt,
One crime.
I say crime, but is it really a crime to taste such fruit?

The fruit has brought good to us both directly and indirectly,
As it has provided an opportunity for us to test and prove our love.
If I thought that death was coming,
I would insist on enduring the worst alone.
I wouldn't let you die with me.
For I know that it would disturb your heart to think of death.
But I don't think death will be the result.
The result will be a greater life
And opened eyes,
New hopes,
New joys,
And a taste of something so delicious
That whatever I ate before seems flat and harsh.
Trust me, Adam.
Taste freely
And cast all fear of death to the winds.

Narrator:

Eve threw herself into Adam's arms and wept for joy
Because she understood his great love for her.
She saw that he would endure the displeasure of God for her sake,
Even to the point of death.
She freely gave him the enticing fruit.
Adam took it and ate,
Although he was not deceived.
He knew it was wrong,
But he was overcome with Eve's charms.
The Earth trembled deep inside its core,
As though it were about to give birth to nature all over again.
The clouds drew close to the ground
And the thunder rumbled.
Sad raindrops fell,
Weeping at the fulfillment of sin.
Mortal sin.
Original sin.
Adam ate his fill,
And Eve joined him in his meal.

They felt like they were drunk.
Laughter seized them.
They felt the divine growing within them,
Almost as though they were growing wings to fly to the heavens
And look down on the Earth with scorn.
But the fruit did something else to them as well.
Adam looked at Eve with lustful desire,
And Eve eyed Adam in the same way.
Together they burned in lust
Until Adam began to seduce Eve.

Adam:

I see now what good taste you have, Eve.
You have great wisdom.
I see that our pleasures also will be increased by this fruit.
I give you much praise for how well this day has turned out.
We missed a lot of pleasure because we didn't eat this fruit sooner.
Until now, we haven't known true tasting and true delight.
If this is the kind of pleasure we get from forbidden things,
Then I wish there were ten forbidden trees instead of only one.
But come to me.
Let us play together as is fitting after such delicious food.
Your beauty never made me feel like this before.
That is one of the great gifts of this Tree.

Narrator:

Adam's eyes roved over Eve's body.
Eve understood and looked at him with blazing eyes.
He grabbed her by the hand
And led her to a shady bank,
Overhung with a roof of greenery.
They lay upon the flowers,
Pansies, violets, asphodel, and hyacinth
And took their fill of love.
In doing so, they sealed their mutual guilt,

And were comforted in their sin.
Finally, exhausted, they fell asleep.

The aroma of the fruit wafted about them as they slept.
They slept heavily.
Nightmares weighed them down.
Finally, they rose but had slept poorly.
They looked at each other
And found that their eyes were now opened
And their minds were darkened.
The innocence that had protected them from evil was gone.
They had no more natural righteousness,
No more honor,
Only naked and guilty shame.
Adam covered himself,
But his covering exposed more than his nakedness did.
It was like when Samson arose from loving the harlot Delilah
And found he had lost his strength.
They sat for a long time silently,
Stripped of their virtue
And stricken by their loss.
Finally, Adam said what they were both thinking.

Adam:

Oh Eve! It was an evil hour when you listened to that worm.
He counterfeited man's voice.
Truly we have fallen—not risen to godhood.
Our eyes are open.
We understand good and evil.
Good has been lost to us.
We are left with evil.
If this is what it means to know,
If this is what it means to have knowledge,
Being stripped of all our honor, innocence, faith, and purity,
Then the eating was evil indeed.
Even our faces show the signs of our foul guilt.
The last evil to come upon us is shame.

How shall I ever look God in the face again?
Or even the angels?
Before, to look on angels was a great joy to me.
But now, even looking is impossible.
Their brightness will blind me should I try.
I wish I could live here as a beast,
Hidden in some shadowy wood
Where the light of the Sun and Stars cannot penetrate.
Cover me, oh pines and cedars!
Hide me with your innumerable boughs
So I never have to look to the Heavens again!
But let's figure out now
How to hide the shameful parts of ourselves from each other.
If we get leaves from a broad-leaved tree
And sew them together,
We can put them about our middle parts
And cover our shame,
Because right now they're visible
And telling us we are unclean.

Narrator:

This was his advice.
So together they went into the thickest wood
And chose the fig tree.
It wasn't the regular fig tree that is known for its fruit,
But the Indian fig,
Which has broad and long branches.
Its branches take root in the ground
So that daughter trees grow about the mother tree
And make a dome arching above the ground.
It was those leaves they gathered.
They sewed them together clumsily.
They wore the leaves around their waists,
Trying in vain to cover their shame and guilt.
Oh, how unlike their first naked glory it was!
They had done their best to cover their shame,
But their minds could not rest,

And they sat down and wept.
It wasn't only tears raining down on their faces and in their hearts.
A more insidious storm rose up in each of them,
Bringing anger, hate, mistrust, suspicion, discord, and passions
To shake their inmost minds,
Which were once the realm of peace.
Understanding and will were now subject to sensual appetites.
Those appetites rose up and took the place of reason and logic.
From his newly bent soul,
Adam, who wasn't himself anymore, spoke again to Eve.

Adam:

You should have listened to me before all this happened.
I don't know what possessed you to go off on your own
When I asked you directly to stay with me.
If you had listened, we would still be happy.
But now we're ruined.
We've lost all that was good,
We're shamed, naked, and miserable.
I have no more reason to trust you.
In trusting you, I have failed myself.

Eve, feeling blamed:

What you've said is severe, Adam.
You're blaming me for wandering,
But the same thing might have happened if we were together.
Or it might have happened to you alone.
You wouldn't have known the serpent was lying.
He spoke well,
And he'd never been a known enemy.
There was no reason for him to hurt me.
Was I supposed to never leave your side?
If so, then I may as well still be one of your ribs.
And if you think I'm so lowly,
Why didn't you just command me outright not to go
If you knew all along it was so dangerous?

You let me go.
You allowed it.
You even approved it.
If you had been firm and solid in your disagreement,
I would have stayed and neither one of us would have sinned.

Adam, outraged:

You ingrate!
I didn't have to fall with you.
I chose to fall with you because I loved you,
And because I didn't want to ever be parted from you!
I might have had eternal life and bliss,
But I chose to die with you.
Are you now trying to say it's my fault?
What else could I have done?
I warned you.
I admonished you.
I told you danger was lurking.
Using force would have been wrong,
For you were free.
But you were confident.
You didn't think you would meet danger,
Or else you thought the trial would be glorious to you.
My only error was in thinking you were so perfect.
I didn't think evil had a chance with you.
I regret making that mistake now,
Because now you're blaming me for the whole thing.
That's what happens when men let women make the decisions.
Women have no restraint,
And left to themselves will blame anything that happens on a man.

Narrator:

They spent hours arguing and accusing each other.
Neither one took responsibility for the crime.
It seemed their argument would never end.

BOOK 10: PART 1

God confronts Adam and Eve and pronounces His judgment.
Death and Sin make their way to Earth.

Narrator:

All Heaven knew what they had done
And what Satan had done,
How the serpent had corrupted Eve and her husband.
Nothing can escape the eye of God, the all-seeing.
Nothing can deceive God's all-knowing heart.
God is wise and just.
He didn't stop Satan from testing the mind of man.
Man was strong.
Man had free will.
He had what he needed to stand against any enemy.
Despite the trickery of their enemy,
Adam and Eve should still have known
Not to taste the fruit,
No matter what.
They didn't obey, and so they earned the punishment for themselves.
They were full of sin.
They deserved to fall.

The angels who guarded Paradise
Flew up to Heaven in a hurry.
They were sad for man
For they saw that he had fallen.
Because of this, they knew the enemy had gotten past them.

As soon as the news arrived in Heaven,
All who heard it were upset.
Even Heavenly faces can be sad.
But that sadness is mixed with pity,

And it doesn't mean they have stopped rejoicing.
Everyone ran to the angel guards to hear what had happened.
The angel guards went quickly to the throne of God.
They explained what happened.

God did not blame them.
He spoke in a voice like thunder.

God the Father:

Angels and Angel Guards!
Do not be dismayed by this news from Earth.
Nothing you could have done would have prevented it.
I told you back when we saw the tempter leave Hell
That he would have success on his mission.
I knew man would be seduced into believing lies about his Maker.
Nothing I did made him fall.
I gave him free will—and her as well.
But now he is fallen,
And all I have left to do is pronounce the sentence of death.
He thinks death is not coming
Because he didn't die as soon as he ate the fruit.
But by nightfall, he will know that we have not overlooked his sin.
Justice shall prevail.

But whom shall I send to judge them?
None other than my Son,
My co-ruler.
I have given Him the power of all judgment
On Heaven and on Earth and in Hell.
You can clearly see that I intend to give mercy as well as judgment,
For I am sending my Son, man's mediator,
His Ransom and willing Redeemer,
The One destined to become a man,
To pronounce the judgment.

Narrator:

As God the Father spoke,
A blaze of glorious light fell on His Son.
He was the full image of the Father.

God the Son:

Eternal Father, it is yours to command
And mine to obey.
I want you always to be pleased with me.
I am going now to judge these sinners.
But I know that whatever the punishment is,
It must fall on me instead when the time comes,
For I told you I would do it.
I am not sorry I took on this task.
I will soften their doom by taking it on myself.
I will bring them mercy in the middle of judgment.
No one needs to come with me.
No one needs to hear my judgment
Except the two who are being judged.
The third lawbreaker has fled,
But he is condemned all the same.
We don't need any proof of error for the serpent.

Narrator:

After He said this, the Son rose from his radiant throne.
The angels accompanied Him to Heaven's gate.
He could see Eden and all the surrounding regions from there.
He went straight down.
Although speed is meaningless to the eternal,
He came down swiftly.
It was afternoon, and the Sun was low in the sky.
Gentle breezes fanned the Earth,
Ushering in the cool of evening.
It was then that the Son came,
Judge and intercessor both,

To pronounce the sentence on Man.
Adam and Eve heard the voice of God in the garden.
The soft winds brought it to their ears.
They heard it, and they hid in the thickest trees,
Until God, approaching, called to Adam.

God the Son:

Where are you, Adam?
You usually come to meet me joyfully.
I don't see you anywhere.
You used to come without me calling to you,
But I'm here now and find myself alone.
Did I come too quietly this time?
Or did something change for you?
Did something happen to delay you?
Come here!

Narrator:

Adam came, and with him came Eve.
They were both upset.
They didn't want to offend Him.
There was no love in the looks they gave to God
Or to each other.
The only thing reflected in their faces
Was guilt and shame and trouble,
Anger and stubbornness,
Hate and deception.
After Adam fumbled for speech, he answered briefly.

Adam:

I heard You in the garden.
I was naked, so I was afraid and hid myself.

God the Son:

You have heard my voice often
And it has never made you afraid.
You are usually glad to see me.
How have I become dreadful to you?
Who told you that you were naked?
Have you eaten the fruit of the Tree?
The fruit I commanded you not to eat?

Adam, agitated:

Oh Heaven!
I stand before my judge today in a bad place.
I either have to take the blame for the whole crime,
Or accuse my other half, my wife, my partner.
Because she is my wife, I shouldn't blame her.
But I can't do that.
If I try to hide the truth, you will know it.
This woman You gave me as a helper,
Who was supposed to be a perfect gift,
So good and fitting and acceptable,
So divine that I would never expect anything bad to come from her,
This woman gave me the fruit and I ate.

God the Son, to Adam:

Is she your god?
Is that what made you choose to obey her?
Is she your guide?
Is she superior to you, or even equal to you?
Is that why you resigned your manhood
And the place of authority God gave you?
Your perfections were greater than hers.
She was beautiful.
God made her lovely so you would fall in love with her,
Not so you would become subject to her.
God gave her talents that were perfectly suited to her position

As one who is ruled, but not as a ruler.
Ruling was your job.
You knew that.

God the Son, to Eve:

Woman, what have you done?

Eve, ashamed:

The serpent tricked me, and I ate.

Narrator:

When the Son heard this,
He did not delay in pronouncing judgment on the serpent,
Even though snakes are just animals.
Punishing a snake cannot bring punishment to Satan.
By possessing the serpent,
Satan destroyed its nature.
This is something man cannot understand and does not need to.
But God pronounced a dual judgment
On both Satan and the serpent.

God the Son, to the serpent:

Because you have done this,
You are the most cursed of all the animals.
You shall grovel on your belly
Eating dust all the days of your life.
I will put animosity between you and the woman,
And between her offspring and you.
Her seed shall bruise your head,
And you shall bruise his heel.

Narrator:

The prophecy was verified
When he saw Satan fall out of Heaven like lightning.

He was called the prince of the air.
Jesus the son of Mary, who was the second Eve,
Rose from the grave
To ruin Principalities and Powers.
The realm of Satan had been conquered long before,
And at last, He shall tread Satan under our feet.
This was the same Jesus
Who predicted the fatal bruise to the head of the serpent.

God the Son, to Eve:

You will bring forth children in sorrow.
You will submit to your husband's will.
He will rule over you.

God the Son, to Adam:

Because you listened to your wife and ate of the forbidden Tree,
Cursed is the ground.
The ground shall bring forth thorns and thistles.
Only by hard labor shall you raise any plants for food.
By the sweat of your brown, you will eat bread.
Know and understand what you are.
You are dust and you shall return to dust.

Narrator:

In this way, the Son judged Man.
He was both Judge and Savior.
He delayed the death sentence.
He looked at them in pity.
He was the same One who washed His servants' feet.

Now, as the Father of His family,
He clothed them with animal skins.
Were the animals killed for their skins?
Or did they shed the skin like snakes,
Thinking nothing of their sacrifice?

He didn't only clothe them on the outside.
He covered their inward nakedness
With His robe of righteousness,
So that the Father above would not look on them.

Then He returned to His Father
And took up His everlasting glory.
He knew what had happened to Man,
And He interceded for him.

Meanwhile, before the sin and the judgment on Earth,
Sin and Death sat,
One at each side of the open gates of Hell.
Outrageous flames belched forth from Hell,
Stretching through the chaos.
Then Sin spoke to Death.

Sin:

Oh my son, why are we sitting here idly
While Satan, our author, is living in another world?
We would be happier there with him.
I'm sure he's had success there.
If things had gone wrong, he would have returned by now
Full of fury and chased by his avengers.

I feel new strength rising inside me.
I feel that I must have been given power far beyond this deep place.
Something is tugging at me like a magnet.
Something out there makes me want to move toward it.
Something like me is out there.
You are my shadow and must come with me,
For nothing can separate Sin from Death.

Maybe it's taking so long for Satan to return
Because it's difficult to cross this enormous gulf.
It would be hard work to make a path from Hell to the new world,
But we have the ability to do so.

After all, Satan rules there now.
We could build a road between here and there.
It would be a glorious monument.
It would be a help to all the demons.
Then any of them could go there.
It will be easy to find.
I'm drawn there strongly by instinct and attraction.

Death:

Go, then.
I will follow.
I can smell the carnage from here.
My prey awaits, and I'm eager for a taste of what lives there.
I won't shirk my share of the work either.
I'll help you in the task.

Narrator:

After he said this, Death sniffed the air with delight.
He could smell the mortal change that had happened on Earth.
Like a vulture, he knew the death of humanity was near.
Death turned his nostrils high into the murky air.
He understood his prey from afar.

Then both Death and Sin flew from the gates of Hell
Into the anarchy of chaos.
They hovered powerfully over the waters
And stirred up the matter, tossing it up and down.
They crowded the elements together,
Like when two waves of the sea join and make a mountain.
Death took his stony mace
And whacked the cold, dry soil until it was hard.
He stared at the rest of the material,
Immobilizing it with his gaze.
The bridge was as broad as the gates of Hell.
They fixed its roots in Hell
And fastened it over the chasm between Hell and Earth.

On they worked, building an arch over the foaming deep,
A bridge of fantastic length.
The new world now had no protection from Death.
From that time on, there was a broad passage,
A smooth and easy road down to Hell.
Once they finished, all three places were connected:
Heaven,
Hell,
Earth.

BOOK 10 PART 2 REFERENCES

Amphisbaena *(animal):* Mythical snake with a head at both ends.

Cerastes *(animal):* Mythical horned snake that hides itself in the sand with only its horns protruding in order to lure prey.

Dipsas *(animal):* Mythical snake whose bite would cause extreme thirst

Ellops *(animal):* Mythical sea serpent; can also be spelled Elops

Furies *(goddesses):* Ancient Greek goddesses of vengeance

Hydrus *(animal):* Mythical creature that, when eaten by a crocodile, would eat its way out, killing the crocodile. Most often depicted as a kind of water snake, but also believed by some to be an otter, an eel, or a bird.

BOOK 10: PART 2

Satan and the demons are judged.
God initiates His plan of salvation.
Adam and Eve repent.

Narrator:

Then they turned toward Paradise.
They saw Satan, in the likeness of a bright angel
Standing among the Stars on the dark side of the Earth.
He was disguised as an angel,
But his dear children knew him.
After he seduced Eve, he crept into the woods nearby
And changed shape
And waited to see what would happen.
He saw Eve present the fruit to her husband.
He saw Adam and Eve try to cover their shame with leaves.

But when he saw the Son of God descend to judge them,
He was terrified and fled.
He knew he'd never get away,
But he could delay what was coming to him
And hopefully avoid the worst of His wrath.
In the night, after the judgment was over,
He returned and listened to Adam and Eve moan and complain.
He learned that his doom was not coming right away,
But would come to him in the future.
Joyfully, he started on his journey back to Hell.
Once he came to the bridge
He met his offspring, Death and Sin.
They were glad to see each other
And he was filled with joy at the sight of the bridge.
He admired it for a long time
Until Sin, his enchanting daughter, broke the silence.

Sin:

Oh my parent, this bridge is your doing, your trophy,
Even though you don't see it that way yet.
You are its author and architect.
My heart is in harmony with yours.
When I understood your victory on Earth,
I knew I had to come here, to follow you
And bring your son, Death, as well.
We three belong together.
Hell could no longer hold us.
You have won our freedom.
We were trapped inside Hell until now.
You gave us power and strength
To build this massive bridge over the dark abyss.
All this new world is yours now.
Your talents have won this for you.
What your hands could not build,
You achieved by your wisdom.

We lost the war for Heaven,
But here you are the king.
Let God rule in Heaven as the battle has judged.
But let Him leave this new world.
He has lost it.
Let Him sharply divide his realm from yours
Or he will find you even more threatening to His throne.

Satan, happily:

Fair daughter, Sin,
And Death, who is both my son and grandson,
You prove yourselves to be my children.
For my name is Satan, which means enemy of Heaven,
And I glory in it.
It is fitting that you have brought the infernal empire
So close to the door of Heaven.
Your victory and mine meet at this place.

Hell and Earth are now one realm,
One continent,
With a highway going through it.
I'm going to take this road you've built.
I'm going down to the darkness.
I want to let the others know about my success,
So we can rejoice together.

You two should go straight to Paradise.
Stay there and rule happily.
Have dominion over all the Earth
And chiefly over Man,
Who has been declared the Earth's ruler.
Make it a priority to win his heart
And later to kill him.
I send you as my ambassadors.
You will rule on Earth by the power that I have gained.
My grip on this new kingdom depends on your performance.
If you prevail, then Hell has nothing to fear.

Narrator:

Satan dismissed them.
They went quickly through the constellations, spreading their evil.
The Stars became pale.
Each Planet was stricken and suffered a real eclipse.

Satan went the other way,
Down the bridge to Hell's gates.
He went through the gate,
Which was wide open and unguarded.
Lucifer was what they called Satan.
Lucifer means light,
And Satan presented himself as a bright morning Star.

At the walls of Pandemonium, the legions kept watch for him,
Just as he'd ordered them as he left.
He came and passed among them

Disguised as a plain angel of the lowest order.
No one saw him as he came into the hall.
He was invisible to them as he ascended his luxurious throne.
He sat for a while, unseen.
After some time, his head materialized as out of a cloud.
The shape of a bright Star appeared.
It was brighter than it had been before the fall,
Shining forth with false glitter.
They were all amazed at the sudden light.
They turned toward it suddenly.
They saw what they wished to see—
Their leader had returned.
They praised him loudly.
The advisors rushed forward,
And joyfully congratulated him.
Satan held up his hand for silence and spoke to them.

Satan:

Thrones, Dominions, Princedoms, Virtues, and Powers!
I declare that I have been wildly successful.
I have returned to lead you triumphantly out of this infernal pit.
For it is abominable and cursed,
A house of woe and a tyrant's dungeon.
Now you shall possess and rule over a spacious world.
It is not much smaller than Heaven itself.
I have won it by my own deeds and in great danger.
It would be a long story if I told it—
What I did,
How I suffered,
How brutal the journey over the deep was.

But now Sin and Death have paved a broad way over it
To make your glorious march easy for you.
But I took on the burden of the journey without a road.
I rode on the abyss.
I plunged into original night and wild chaos.
In this way, I found the newly created world.

I found a creation of absolute perfection.
Man was there, placed in Paradise.
He was happy because we were in exile.
I seduced him from his Creator by fraud.
And better yet, I did it with an apple.
You should laugh at God now.
He had to give up his beloved man and all the new world.
It is now the prey of Sin and Death.
We can live and rule there,
Even though man was supposed to rule Earth.

I guess it's fair to say that God pronounced judgment on me also.
Well, not on me exactly,
But on the serpent whose shape I was wearing when I deceived Man.
The curse was this:
That he would make us enemies, me and mankind.
I am to bruise his heel.
His seed will bruise my head.
That's all I had to give to acquire a world.
It was well worth it.
That is my story.
There is nothing else to do but to go up to Earth
And enter that happy place together.

Narrator:

Having said this, Satan expected shouts of praise and much applause.
But instead, he heard a dismal hiss from every tongue.
It was the sound of public scorn.
He was shocked—but not for long.
He felt his face narrow and become thin.
His arms became welded to his ribs.
His legs twined about each other.
Finally, having no limbs to hold him up, he fell.
He was a monstrous serpent lying on its belly.

It wasn't Satan who had the power now.
He took the form of a snake when he sinned.

He was being punished by being confined to that shape,
For such was his doom.
He would have spoken again,
But he could only hiss.

There were hisses all around
As all were transformed into serpents.
All were punished as accessories to his crime.
The sound of hissing filled the hall with dreadful noise.
The hall was swarming with monsters now—

     Scorpions.
         Asps.
             Amphisbaena.
                  Cerastes.
                       Hydrus.
                           Ellops.
                               Dipsas.

But still Satan was the greatest among them.
He grew up into the form of a dragon,
A huge python who would rule the rest.

They followed him to an open field
Where all the other demons were waiting.
They expected to see their glorious leader emerging in triumph.
They saw something else instead—
A crowd of ugly serpents.
They were horrified, both with terror and sympathy.
As they saw it, they began to change also.
They dropped their spears and shields
And fell on the ground beside them and began to hiss.
It was like the change was contagious.
Their triumph turned to shame.

Beside them stood a grove of trees,
Which had sprung up while they were changing.
It was God's will to set it there

To make their punishment worse.
The trees were like the Tree in Paradise,
The one Satan had used to tempt Eve.
They all marveled at this strange sight.
In Paradise there was one tree.
Here there were many,
Given to bring them more woe and shame.

The demons were parched with scalding thirst
And they were fiercely hungry.
They knew the trees were sent to bring punishment to them
But they couldn't help themselves.
They slithered up the trees and sat among the branches
Like the snaky hair of Medusa.
Greedily they plucked the best-looking fruit.
The fruit looked good,
But in their mouths, it turned to bitter ashes.
They spat it out of their mouths.
They kept trying the fruit because they were so hungry.
But every time they tried, their jaws writhed
As they bit down on soot and cinders.
Man fell once.
The demons fall continually.
They were tormented like this,
Worn out with hunger,
Always hissing.

Some say that this happens to them once a year,
Being made into serpents.
This is to humble them
And slam them for the pride they feel over mankind's destruction.

The hellish pair—Sin and Death—arrived in Paradise.
Sin's power was there before,
But now she was there herself
Ready to live there forever.
Death followed her closely
But not yet riding his pale horse.

Sin:

Oh second child of Satan,
All-conquering Death,
What do you think of our empire now?
Although we had to work so hard for it,
Isn't it better than sitting at the gate of Hell
Watching and nameless and starved?

Death:

To me it's all the same—
Hell or Paradise or Heaven.
I prefer whichever one gives me the most food.
To me, it doesn't seem like there's much here to stuff my face with.

Sin:

Well, eat these herbs and fruits and flowers first.
Then eat the animals and fish and birds.
They're moderately tasty, and they must die sometime.
Eat all of them as you please.
I'll concentrate on Man.
I'll ooze into his thoughts, looks, words, and actions.
I'll infect them with myself,
Until he is well-seasoned
And ready to be the most savory prey.

Narrator:

Then they began their destruction.
They ate some creatures immediately.
Others, they made mortal.
They wanted to make all of them proceed toward destruction.

God saw this from His throne above,
And He spoke.

God the Father:

See what waste and destruction these Dogs of Hell are making
Of the world which I made beautiful and good?
I kept it beautiful and good,
But Man's sin has let in these wasteful Furies.
They turn all I have created into foolishness.
They have that right
Because I have allowed them to enter and possess Paradise.
They think I must be on their side.
To them it seems like I've given up,
And they laugh.
They don't know that it was I who called them here.
They're my Hellhounds.
I chose them to lick up the filth of man's polluting sin.
They will gorge themselves until they are about to burst
Because their guts are so full of excrement.
At one stroke of your victorious arm, My Son,
Sin and Death and the yawning grave
Will at last be hurled through chaos
Into the mouth of Hell
And sealed up there forever.
Then Heaven and Earth will be renewed and made pure.
Mankind will no longer be stained by sin.
But until then, the curse is in effect.

Narrator:

At this, the heavenly audience sang hallelujahs.
It sounded like the sea.
They sang, "Just are Your ways.
Righteous are Your decrees on all Your works.
Who can make You less than You are?"

Then they sang to the Son,
The one destined to restore mankind
And by whose power the new Heaven and new Earth shall arise,
Or descend from Heaven, as the case may be.

While they sang, God called His angels by name,
Giving them tasks just right for that moment.

The Sun was given orders first.
He was to move and shine on the Earth,
Bringing both cold and heat that were barely tolerable.
He was to bring icy, frigid winter in the North,
And the fiery heat of summer in the South.
He gave the white Moon its job.
He told the other five Planets their regularity of movement
That has a harmful influence on the Earth.
He told the Stars when to shower down judgment
And how they should cause distress.
He gave the winds their corners
And told them when to stir up the sea, air, and shore.
He told the thunder when to bring terror to the dark halls of the sky.

Some say He commanded His angels to tip the Earth
So that its poles were not aligned with the axle of the Sun.
It was hard work to turn the upright Earth on an angle.
Others say it was the Sun that turned from its road around the Earth
To follow the path of the constellations of the zodiac.
This is what brings the changing of the seasons.
If it had not turned, it would have been spring forever on Earth,
With days and nights equal in length
Except to those at the poles.
At the poles it is always day,
As though the Sun was making up for being so far from them.

Although these changes in the Heavens were slow,
They produced similar changes in the sea and land—
Blasts from the Stars,
Vapor,
Mist,
Hot, earthy breaths,
corrupt and foul.

Next, from the northern parts of the Earth
The four winds burst from their dungeons
Armed with ice and snow,
Hail and stormy winds.
They tore apart the woods and upset the seas.
Black, thunderous clouds fiercely rush,
Making all manner of noise.

Thus began the outrage of the lifeless parts of creation.
Discord is the first offspring of Sin.
Animals began to fight with each other.
Instead of eating plants,
They began to eat each other.
They didn't respect man anymore.
They fled from him or glared at him.

Adam saw these growing miseries
Even though he was hiding in the gloomiest shade.
He had given himself over to despair.

Adam:

Everything that used to be happy is miserable.
Is this the end of this glorious new world?
I used to be the glory of God's glory,
But now I am cursed.
Hide me from the face of God.
Seeing the face of God used to be my greatest joy.
It would be good if He would end this misery right here.
I deserve it.
I want it.
But it will not happen.
Everything I eat or drink or beget is cursed.
I once thought it was a delight to be told to have children.
Now it is death to me.
For what can I beget but more curses?
My children will feel the evil I brought on them
And will curse my head.

Everything I beget will come back to hurt me.
I am the center, and the curse will fall on me.
Oh fleeting joys of Paradise!
I paid for you with lasting sorrow.
Did I ask you, my Maker, to make me into a man?
Did I ask you to bring me into the light
And set me in a delicious garden?
I had nothing to do with it.
You could return me to dust.
It is Your right.
I wish I could return to dust
And give back to You all You gave me.
I couldn't do what You asked.
I couldn't hold onto the good You gave me.
It would have been justice.
Why have you added all these endless woes?
Your justice is inexplicable.
It's too late for me to complain.

I should have refused your terms when you gave them.
But I didn't.
I accepted them.
Now He is punishing me as I deserve.

What if my own son turns out to be disobedient
And asks why I begat him?
What if he says, "I didn't ask to be born."
Am I going to let him off the hook?
God made me by His own choice,
And He wanted me to serve Him.
I was given a reward for it because He is gracious.
I am punished justly, as He wills.
Let it be done.
I submit.
My doom is fair.
I am dust, and to dust I will return.
I welcome it whenever it happens.

Why is His hand delaying the punishment?
Why have I lived so long?
Why is death mocking me,
Stretching out the punishment into endless pain?
I would gladly meet death and return to the earth.
It would be like laying down as in my mother's lap.
I would rest there and sleep.
His dreadful voice would stop thundering in my ears.
I would no longer be tormented by fears
Of what was going to happen to me and my offspring.
I have only one fear left—
That I cannot die.

What if the breath of life—my soul—cannot perish with my body?
Then, in the grave or someplace worse,
I shall die a living death.
What a horrid thought if it's true!
It was the breath of life—my soul—that sinned.
Therefore, it should be the soul that dies.
The body doesn't have breath.
It doesn't have a soul.
All of me should die, not just my body.

God is the Lord of all infinity.
Is His wrath also infinite?
Even if His wrath is infinite, man isn't.
He is doomed to death.
How can God exercise wrath without end
On a man who will eventually die?
Will His wrath keep going after I am dead?
For the sake of His anger will he make the finite infinite?
Will this satisfy his wrath?
That would be to extend the sentence of death
Beyond death and dust and the laws of nature.
Everything else acts according to its nature.
But what if death is not a single stroke like I think it is?
What if instead of just making me nothing,
It subjects me to endless misery from now on?

What if it goes on forever?
Ay me! That fear comes thundering over me,
That both death and I are eternal and spiritual.
And it wouldn't just be me,
But all my children and children's children would be cursed.
What a great inheritance to leave for my sons!
I wish I could take it all on myself and leave none for you, my sons.
If I disowned you now, you would thank me.
Why should all mankind be condemned for one man's fault?
They didn't do anything.
But what can come out of me now but evil ones,
Bent in both mind and will?
They will not only do what I did,
They will desire to do what I did.
How will they be able to stand before God as innocent?
Therefore, I conclude that God is just.
All my rationalizations and evasions
Only lead me back to the same answer.
I am the source of corruption.
All blame lands on me.
I deserve the wrath of God.

I wish I could share the burden with that bad woman.
And even in this, the thing I desire destroys me.
There is no refuge.
I am miserable.
The only one comparable to me is Satan.
My conscience drives me into an abyss of fears and horrors!
There is no way out.
I only plunge deeper and deeper in.

Narrator:

Adam lamented all night long.
Night was not like it was before the fall,
Wholesome and cool and mild.
It was full of black air, damp, and gloom.
Adam's conscience caused him to view these things with terror.

He lay stretched out on the cold ground
And cursed the creation.
He cursed Death for taking so long to claim him.
He cursed the day he sinned.

Adam:

Why doesn't Death come and end me with one stroke?
Shall truth fail to keep her word?
Won't justice hurry up?
But Death doesn't come when you call it.
Justice doesn't hurry for anyone.
Oh woods, oh fountains,
Oh hills and valleys and bowers,
I taught you to sing this wretched song.

Narrator:

Eve saw that he was full of despair.
She came near and tried to speak softly to him.
He turned her away sternly.

Adam:

Get out of my sight, you serpent!
That's the best name for you, for the serpent is your ally.
You are a hateful traitor.
The only differences between you and the serpent
Are your shape and color.
I wish you'd turn into one, so all creatures would be warned.
Otherwise, your heavenly form will deceive them.
If it weren't for you, I would have stayed happy.

You criticized me for not trusting you.
But the serpent fooled and seduced you.
And you fooled and seduced me.
It was foolish to trust you so far away from me.
I thought you were wise, steadfast, and mature.

I thought you could stand against all assaults.
I didn't understand that it was just a show.
Everything about you except the one rib is crooked and bent.
It would be better if my rib had been discarded.
I probably had extras anyway.
God made the angels of Heaven male.
Why did He make this novelty on Earth?
Why make a woman at all, beautiful as she is?
Why couldn't he have found
Some other way for mankind to reproduce?
Then this evil would not have happened.
And even more evil is coming directly from the females.
A man will either not be able to find a wife
Because women are so contrary,
Or because her parents object to her loving him,
Or he will find a woman,
But she will be already married to his enemy.

Narrator:

He stopped talking and turned away.
Eve fell at his feet, with tears streaming down her face
And her hair all mussed.
She hugged his feet and begged for him to be at peace with her.
Then she made her complaint.

Eve:

Don't forsake me like this, Adam!
Let Heaven be my witness how much I love and respect you.
I didn't mean to offend you.
I didn't mean to deceive you.
I am your servant.
Don't make me grieve.
You are my life,
With your gentle looks, your help,
And your counsel in my distress.
You are my strength and my hope.

Without you, where will I go? What will I do?
While we are still alive,
Which might not be for long,
Let us join together in peace against our enemy, the serpent.
Don't hate me because of what has happened.
I'm more miserable than you.
We both sinned, but you only sinned against God.
I sinned against both God and you.
I beg Heaven to remove the judgment from you
And give it to me alone.
I'm the cause of all this misery.
I should be the one to receive God's wrath.

Narrator:

She stopped weeping.
Adam heard her confession and sorrow,
And soon his heart softened toward her.
After all, it wasn't that long ago that she was his life and his delight.
Now she knelt at his feet looking for his forgiveness.
She was so beautiful.
His anger seeped away, and with peaceful words, he lifted her up.

Adam:

You are reckless.
It's foolish to want the whole punishment to fall on yourself.
Bear your own punishment alone.
You can barely endure having me angry with you.
God's full wrath will be much worse.
If prayers could change things,
I would quickly pray in a louder voice than you
That God would lay all His wrath on my head.
I would ask Him to forgive you
Because of the frailty and weakness of the female sex.
You were given to me to take care of.
It is my fault you were vulnerable to attack.
But let's not argue any more.

Let's not blame each other.
Let us strive toward love,
So we can lighten each other's burdens.
It looks like Death won't be sudden,
But a slow-paced evil,
In order to make our pain greater.
And it will fall on our children as well.

Eve:

Adam, I know how little my words mean to you
Knowing how wrong I was.
Nevertheless, because you have restored me to your side,
And accepted me, even though I am vile,
And given me hope that I might win back your love,
Which is my heart's only comfort in death or in life,
I will not hide from you the thoughts in my heart.

I'm pondering how we can get some relief
Or how we can die more quickly.
The most worrisome thing is our children.
They will be born evil.
Death will devour them in the end.
How miserable it is to be the cause of their misery!
Therefore, we should not conceive children.
We are childless. We ought to stay that way.
Then Death would not get his feast.
He'd have to satisfy himself with only the two of us.

Or if you think it's too awful to live without making love,
Let's try to die right away.
Let's seek Death.
If we can't find him, we should do his job for him.
Why stand here shivering in our fears?
We have the power to choose the method by which we die.
Let's pick the shortest one.

Narrator:

Her cheeks were pale because of her thoughts of death.
But Adam was not swayed by her advice.
He had higher hopes.

Adam:

Neither of these things will work.
You would regret losing your life.
And you love pleasure too much to never make love.
Don't be deceived.
Death won't end your misery or God's punishment.
God is wiser than you know.
I'm afraid that Death will not get us out of this.
If we snatch at death, God will be provoked.
He will make death live in us.
Let's find a safer solution.

I have a thought.
Remember the part of our sentence
Where it was said that
Your seed shall crush the serpent's head?
I think by the serpent, God meant Satan.
Crushing his head would be a good revenge.
We won't get that if we kill ourselves
Or if we never have children, like you suggested.
Our enemy shall escape the punishment that was ordained for him.
Don't speak again of killing ourselves.
Don't speak again of willful childlessness.
That would cut us off from hope
And display rebellion toward God.

Remember how mildly and graciously He spoke to us.
We expected to be dissolved.
We thought we were going to die that day.
But you were given only pains in childbearing.
And once you have a child, you will have joy.

The curse given to me fell off and landed on the ground.
I must work with difficulty to earn my bread.
That's not too bad.
Idleness would be worse.
Working will sustain me.
The extremes of cold and heat have come,
But God cared for us and clothed us.
He has pity for us even now.
If we pray, He will hear us.
He is a God of grace and pity.
He will teach us how to survive seasons of rain, ice, hail, and snow,
Which the sky now begins to show us.
We can learn how to gather the Sun's beams
Or how to make a fire by grinding two objects together.
We can use fire to soften the evils
That our own sin has brought on us.
God will instruct us and give us grace when we ask.
We don't need to fear this life.
He will give us many comforts before we turn back into dust.
The best thing we can do
Is to go back to the place where He judged us
And fall before Him in reverence
And confess our faults
And beg His pardon with tears.
We ought to sigh frequently
To show him that we are genuinely sorrowful.
You know Him.
He will relent and turn from his wrath.
Why else would He have been calm
When He should have been so angry?
He intends to give us favor, grace, and mercy.

Narrator:

So they went to the place where God had judged them
And fell on their knees in reverence.
They confessed their sins humbly
And asked His pardon with tears.

BOOK 11 PART 1 REFERENCES

Argus *(giant):* In ancient Greek mythology, Argus is a giant with a hundred eyes who served as a watchman.

Cusco *(place):* The capital of the Inca Empire in Peru and still a major city in that country. Also spelled Cuzco.

Elisha *(man):* Elisha was a Biblical Old Testament prophet who served under the prophet Elijah, and saw his mentor carried off to Heaven in a chariot of fire.

Jacob *(man):* In the Bible, Jacob, later named Israel, was the patriarch of the twelve tribes of Israel. In a dream he had a vision of a ladder reaching to heaven, with angels going up and down. In the dream, God promised him many descendants through whom all the earth would be blessed.

Montezuma *(man):* Emperor of the Aztec Empire in the early 1500s, Montezuma was killed during the Spanish conquest of Mexico.

the Sultan *(man):* Byzantium, the remnant of ancient Rome, was conquered by the Ottoman Empire in 1453 A.D. and was thenceforward (until 1922 A.D.) ruled by a sultan.

BOOK 11: PART 1

Michael visits Adam and Eve in their distress.
He begins to tell them the disastrous future of mankind.

Narrator:

Adam and Eve were praying and repentant.
They had been brought to their lowest point.
God's grace had removed the hardness from their hearts.
He made them new hearts of flesh.
The prayers they breathed were inspired by the Holy Spirit.
Their quiet prayers flew toward Heaven
More quickly than the loudest speeches.
The vagabond winds did not blow aside their prayers
Or interrupt their course.
Their prayers passed through Heaven's doors
To the golden altar.
The Son stood before the Father's throne
And began to intercede for them.

God the Son:

Look, Father, at the result of the grace you have sent.
These prayers have grown from the seed you planted in their hearts.
I bring these prayers before you now, mixed with incense at the altar.
Their repentance is a more pleasing fruit than any fruit in the garden,
For this repentance was born of a sorrowful heart.
Therefore, listen to my plea.
Hear the sighs of Adam even though they are not given in words.
I will tell you what they mean.
I am his advocate.
His works all fall on Me.
My works shall perfect his works.
My death shall pay his price.

Accept Me, and in accepting Me,
Receive the smell of peace toward mankind.
Let him be reconciled to You,
Although his days are numbered
And death will be his doom at the end.
I'm not asking that he avoid death, but that the penalty be softened.
Death will deliver him to a better life.
There, all the redeemed will live with Me in joy and happiness.
They will be one with Me, just as I am one with You.

God the Father:

I will give you what you're asking for.
That was what I intended from the beginning.
But the laws of nature forbid them from staying in Paradise.
He is tainted.
He can't stay where the pure, immortal elements are.
Sin has corrupted what should have been incorruptible.
I gave mankind two beautiful gifts—happiness and immortality.
They tried to find happiness by breaking the Law.
Because of this, they lost both happiness and immortality.
Death is the only cure for a life of hardship.
But that life, refined by faith and faithful works,
Will result in mankind waking to a second life.
Heaven and Earth will be renewed.

But let us call a gathering of all the blessed in Heaven.
I will not hide My judgments from them.
I will tell them My plan for mankind
And for the fallen angels.

Narrator:

The Father ended his speech,
And the Son gave the signal to the minister.
The minister blew his trumpet—the one that sounded
When Moses was given the Ten Commandments
And that will be heard again at the day of judgment.

The angelic blast filled all Heaven.
The sons of light came from all over that beautiful place.
They took their seats before the throne
To hear God pronounce His sovereign will.

God the Father:

Oh my sons,
Man has become like us.
Because he ate the fruit,
He knows both good and evil.
He knows good—but he has lost it.
He is sorry.
He is repentant.
He has asked for mercy.
It is I who have worked these things in him.
Left to himself, his heart is fickle and proud.
We must remove him from the garden
Before he can eat of the Tree of Life.
If he eats of the Tree of Life, he will live forever.
We must send him out to till the soil.
This is the life he deserves now.

Michael, you are in charge.
Choose some warriors from among the cherubim.
Do it before the enemy can make any more trouble.
Hurry and drive the sinful pair out of Paradise.
Proclaim their banishment—and their children's.
But try not to scare them.
I don't want them to faint at the strict sentence.
I have heard their pleas and seen their tears.
If they obey your decree, give them some comfort.
Tell them what shall happen in the future.
Let me tell you what that is:
I will make a covenant with them.
It shall come about through the seed of the woman.
Send them forth with sorrow, but peace as well.
Place a watch at the east side of the garden.

Let cherubs guard the gates with a flaming sword.
They will guard the pathways to the Tree of Life
So that Paradise doesn't become the home of evil
And my trees their prey.

Narrator:

He stopped, and the Archangel prepared to descend,
Taking with him many watchful cherubim.
Each cherub had four faces.
Their forms are covered with more eyes than Argus.
Their eyes aren't prone to falling asleep like his were.
While this was happening, morning dawned,
And fresh dew soothed the earth.
Adam and Eve finished their prayers
And found strength from God,
New hope coming forth from their despair,
Joy, yet linked with fear.

Adam:

Eve, by faith we know that all the good we have is from God.
It's hard to believe that He might notice us,
Or do anything good for us.
But our prayers, and even our very breaths,
Have gone up to the throne of God.
As I prayed with a humble heart,
I thought I saw Him bending to listen to us.
He looked peaceful and mild.
I am sure He will be favorable to us.
I felt peaceful again as I remembered His promise:
Your seed will bruise our enemy.
This assures me that the bitterness of death is past
And we shall live.
Therefore, I greet you, Eve,
Mother of mankind,
Mother of all living things.

For by you, mankind shall live,
And all things live for man.

Eve, sadly:

I'm not worthy to be called the Mother.
I am a sinner.
I was supposed to be your helper
But I became a snare to you.
I should be reprimanded.
I am untrustworthy.
But my Judge is infinitely gracious.
I brought death to all,
Yet I am to be the source of life.
And you have given me the undeserved title of Mother.
But the fields are calling us.
We must work, despite our sleepless night.
The morning doesn't care how tired we are.
Let's go to work. I won't leave you again.
Let's work all day long until the day droops.
This is a pleasant place.
Let us be content here, even though we are fallen.

Narrator:

Eve wished for this good, but it was not to be.
Nature gave the first sign of this with an eclipse.
The eagle looked down on the earth and saw his prey.
The lion began to be a hunter, pursuing deer.
Adam saw this happen and spoke to Eve.

Adam:

Oh Eve, changes are going to happen.
I can see the signs in nature.
We should not be too secure in our release from punishment.
We may have delayed death for the time being,
But who knows how long we will live

Or what our life will be like?
We are dust, and to dust we must return.
Why else would we see the eagle and the lion be hunting?
Why else would the sky be darkened during the day?
And why is there a white cloud in the sky,
Slowly descending from Heaven?

Narrator:

He wasn't wrong about this,
For the white cloud now landed on a hill in Paradise.
It would have been a glorious sight
If Adam's eyes hadn't been clouded by doubt and fear.
It was just as glorious as when Jacob saw the angels descending,
Or when Elisha was surrounded by chariots of fire.
Michael left the angels and went toward Adam alone.
Adam saw him, and when he approached, he spoke to Eve.

Adam:

Eve, now we will find out our destiny.
There may be new laws for us to observe,
For I see one of the angels coming toward us
From the blazing cloud on the hill.
I can tell by the way he walks
That he is one of the great ones.
He is full of majesty.
He is not trying to cause me to fear,
But neither is he friendly like Raphael.
He is solemn and sublime.
I must meet him with reverence.
I must meet him without you.

Narrator:

He stopped speaking,
And the Archangel Michael came near, wearing the form of a man.
He was wearing a purple military vest

Like those worn by kings and heroes of old.
His glittering helmet was unbuckled,
Showing him to be in the prime of manhood.
By his side hung his sword,
Which was the dread of Satan,
And in his hand was a spear.
Adam bowed low.
The angel did not bow in return
But declared his arrival.

Michael:

Adam, your prayers have been heard.
Your due punishment is death,
But it was delayed so you could have time to repent.
The Lord may redeem you from the claws of death.
But you may no longer live in Paradise.
I have come to remove you
And send you out of the garden.
You must work the dirt out of which you were made.
It is more fitting for you.

Narrator:

He stopped there.
Adam was frozen with horror and sorrow at the news.
Eve, who was hiding, heard the news also.
She began to wail aloud.

Eve:

Oh unexpected blow! This is worse than death!
Must I leave Paradise?
Must I leave my native soil,
These happy walks and shady places that are fit for the gods?
I had hoped to stay here,
Quiet and sad,
As I waited out the length of my days.

These flowers can't grow anywhere else.
My little flowers . . .
I have been watching them since their first bud.
I named them myself.
Who shall lift you up to the Sun?
Who shall prune you and bring you water from the fountain?
And my bridal bed!
I put everything sweet and lovely in you.
How shall I leave you behind?
How shall I wander down into the wild and hidden lower world?
How shall we breathe air that is less pure,
When we are used to immortal fruits?

Michael, gently:

Do not lament, Eve.
You must accept this.
It is justice.
Do not set your heart on what doesn't belong to you.
You are not going alone.
Your husband goes with you.
You must follow him and live where he lives.
From now on, that is your native soil.

Adam:

You seem to be the highest of the highest
Because of the gentle way you gave us this message.
It could easily have wounded us unto death.
You have brought more than sorrow and despair.
This place is the only comfort we have left,
And we have to leave it.
We must go to a hostile place.
It is empty and desolate.
It doesn't know us,
Nor do we know it.
If I thought praying would change God's mind,
I would pray without stopping.

But it's useless to pray against a decree of God.
It's no better than breathing into the wind.
Therefore, I submit to God's judgment.

The worst part is that I shall be deprived of God's face.
Here in Eden, I could go here and there,
Visiting the places where God's presence had met me.
I could have told my sons of Him.
He was on this mountain.
He was under this tree.
He was among the pines.
I talked with Him by this fountain.
I would make so many monuments to Him!
Where will I find Him in this new and unknown world?
Although I fled from His anger,
He has still promised to make me the Father of humanity.
I will now see only the farthest reaches of His glory
And see His steps in the distance.

Michael:

Adam, you know Heaven and Earth are His.
His presence fills the land, the sea, and the air.
It fills everything that lives.
Every being is made alive by His power.
He gave you all the Earth to possess and rule.
This is a good gift.
Don't think you can only find God in Eden.
This was meant to be the capital of the world,
The place where all generations would come to worship.
But this future has been lost.
Eden is no longer great.
You are no more than your sons.

But don't doubt that God is out there,
Just as He is here.
You will still see many signs of God's presence.
You will be surrounded by His goodness and fatherly love.

You will see God's divine face
And see His steps
And believe.
Before you leave this place,
I will show you what will come next.
You will see the good and bad that will come.
I will tell you of supernatural grace
Warring with the sinfulness of men.
You will learn patience from it.
You will learn to have fear and sorrow,
Even when you are rejoicing.
You will experience both at once,
Good times and bad.
You will live your life like this.
And in living like that, you will be prepared
To cross over to death when the time comes.
Come up on this hill.
Let Eve sleep below
While I show you what will happen.

Adam:

I will follow you up the path.
I will submit to the hand of Heaven,
Even though it's a hand of chastening.
In suffering, I will overcome.
I will earn rest, if I can.

Narrator:

Both Adam and Michael went up the highest hill of Paradise.
From there, they could see the entire hemisphere of the Earth.
The hill on which Satan tempted Christ in the Bible
Was the same height and width as this one.
Satan tempted Christ, the second Adam,
Showing him all the Earth's kingdoms and their glory,
In order to tempt Him with power.
He showed him all the cities that were or will be:

From the vast greatness of China,
To the great Mogul kingdom in India,
From the throne of the Russian czar in Moscow,
To the Sultan's seat in Byzantium.
He could see the African kingdoms—
Ethiopia, Mozambique, Congo, and Angola.
He could see Morocco, Algeria, and Spain.
He could see Europe, where Rome would rule the world.
He could see Mexico where Montezuma ruled,
And Peru where Cusco sat.
He could see fresh Guiana,
And the city there that is called El Dorado.

Michael removed the veil from Adam's eyes
Which had come upon him when he ate the fruit.
The fruit that promised him clearer sight
Had the opposite effect.
Michael washed Adam's eyes with euphrasy and rue
And dropped water from the well of life into them.
Adam's mental sight was awakened.
It was so bright that he was forced to close his eyes.
He slipped into a trance,
But Michael raised him up and got his attention again.

Michael:

Adam, open your eyes.
See what your crime has brought about.
Your descendants never touched the cursed tree.
They didn't converse with the serpent.
They didn't sin like you did.
But they are corrupt because of your sin.

Narrator:

Adam opened his eyes and saw a field.
It was cultivated land—a farm.
An altar stood there in the grass.

A man came to the altar.
He brought the first fruits of his crops—
A green ear, a yellow sheaf.
He did not pick them specifically,
But took the first crops that came into his hand.

Next came a shepherd.
He humbly brought the best lambs from his flock.
He sacrificed the lambs,
Putting their innards on the altar with incense.

Fire from Heaven consumed the shepherd's offering.
The other man's offering was not consumed.
His offering was not sincerely given.
The man boiled with rage.
He beat the shepherd with a stone
And drove the life out of him.
The shepherd fell, deadly pale
And groaning out his soul with a gush of blood.
Adam was dismayed.

Adam:

Oh Teacher!
Something horrible has happened to that man!
Is this how his piety and devotion are repaid?

Michael, also in dismay:

These are two brothers, Adam.
They are your children.
The unjust has killed the just
Because he was jealous that his brother's offering was accepted.
But he will be avenged.
The shepherd will not lose his reward,
Even though he is rolling in dust and gore.

Adam:

Alas, for both the killing and the jealousy that caused it!
Have I now seen death?
Is this the way I must return to dust?
This is terror, foul and ugly.
It is horrid to think of,
And ugly to see.

Michael:

You have witnessed the first human death.
But there are many kinds of deaths,
And many paths lead to Death's grim cave.
They're all dismal.
Some will die by violence.
More will die by fire, flood, famine, and disease—
A monstrous amount of disease.
You shall see what Eve's sin has brought to men.

Narrator:

Immediately, a place came before his eyes.
It was like a hospital filled with diseased people—
Spasms, torture, agony, fevers,
Convulsions, epilepsy, congestion, intestinal trouble,
Ulcers, colic, demonic frenzy, depression,
Mental illness, atrophy, malnutrition,
Epidemics, edema, asthma, and arthritis.
They tossed and turned.
They groaned in despair.
Death hovered over them without striking,
Although they begged for the relief it would bring.
Who could be so hard-hearted that he wouldn't cry at the sight?
Adam wept, even though he was a man.
Finally, he took hold of himself
And lamented what he had seen.

Adam:

Oh miserable mankind!
It would be better not to be born
Than to endure this wretched state.
Why have life if it's just going to be taken away?
Who would receive life
If he knew how it was going to turn out?
And if he did receive life,
He would soon want it to end.
He'd be glad for a rest at last.
Can men made in the image of God
Be brought so low by pain?
We still bear the image of God.
Shouldn't we be free from horrors like this?

Michael:

The image of God left them
When they served their appetites instead of God.
They became the image of the one they served.
Their punishment is just.
They didn't ruin God's image—
They ruined their own.
They are subject to sickness
Because they had no respect for God's image in themselves.

Adam:

I will agree that it is just.
But isn't there another way?
Can't we come to death without so much pain?

Michael:

There is another way, as you shall see.
Don't eat or drink too much.
Nourish your body, but don't be a glutton.

Then you will have long life.
Then you will be gathered to death like ripe fruit.
But to attain old age,
You must outlive your youth, your strength, and your beauty.
You must become withered and gray.
Your senses will dull.
Pleasures will be gone.
Your longing for hopeful youth will rule you,
And your spirits will be weighed down with depression.
At last, your life will be consumed.

Adam:

I'm not going to flee from Death.
I won't seek to make my life longer.
I will wait all my life patiently
For the day when I may be gathered to God.

Michael:

Don't love your life,
But don't hate it either.
Live well, long or short.
And now, prepare yourself for another sight.

BOOK 11: PART 2

Michael tells Adam the story of Noah and the ark.

Narrator:

Adam looked and saw a wide plain.
It was covered with colored tents.
Herds of cattle grazed.
Harps and organs were playing.
He could see the musicians playing skillfully.
In another area, there was a forge and a blacksmith.
He was working with iron and brass.
He first made his own tools,
And then worked to see what else could be made of metal.
In the west, he saw a group of men coming down from the hills.
They were sturdy men,
Intent on worshipping God and knowing His works,
And trying to preserve freedom and peace among men.
They hadn't been on the plain long
When a group of women came out of the tents.
They were dressed in gems and provocative clothes.
They sung love songs and danced.
The men caressed them with their eyes,
Until at last, they were snared in the women's net of love.
They married the women,
And made love to them all night long.
Songs, flowers, and happiness prevailed.
Adam felt his heart fill with hope and delight.

Adam:

Oh Opener of My Eyes, this vision is much better!
The other things you showed me

Were full of hate and death and pain.
Here I see only fulfillment.

Michael:

Don't judge what's best based on pleasure.
These men were meant for nobler things.
Those are the tents of wickedness.
Remember the man who killed his brother the shepherd?
Those are the tents of his descendants.
Although everything they have came from God,
They do not acknowledge His gifts.
Their life looks good, but they don't think about God.
Although those women are as beautiful as goddesses,
There is no goodness in them.
They exist only to satisfy lust.
They sing, dance, dress, seduce, and flirt.
The men from the hills were religious until they saw the women.
They gave the women all their virtue and fame.
For the sake of pleasure,
They sacrificed themselves to these atheists.
Because of this, the world will weep.

Adam:

Oh what a pity that those who lived well
Turned aside to walk this path.
But I see that things never change.
Man's troubles come from women.

Michael:

The trouble starts from men's laziness.
Men should be wise
Because they were given more gifts from God.
They should know better.
But now I will show you another scene.

Narrator:

Adam saw a wide territory with towns and cities,
Farms and gates and towers.
He saw men with fierce faces
Ready for war.
They were giants, ready for battle.
Some of them rode horses and others went on foot.
A group of men drove the herds forward—
Oxen, cattle, and sheep.
The shepherds called for help
And the bloody battle began.
The field was drenched in blood and then deserted.
Others attacked a city,
Laying siege to it,
Assaulting it,
Fighting with cannons, ladders, and tunnels,
With darts and javelins,
With sulphureous fire.
There were great deeds and slaughter on both sides.
Heralds called an assembly of the council in the city gates.
Arguments were heard, voices rising.

At last, a middle-aged man arose.
He was wise.
He spoke of right and wrong,
Of justice, religion, truth, and peace—
And judgment from above.
The men seized him.
If a cloud hadn't snatched him up to the sky,
He would have been killed.
After that, the violence continued.
There was no refuge.
Adam was in tears.

Adam:
Who are these ministers of Death?
They cannot be men, can they?

They are inhumane,
Multiplying the sin of the one who killed his brother.
They're killing their own brothers!
But who was the good man who was rescued by Heaven?

Michael:

These are the descendants of the godly men
And the children of the man who killed his brother.
They inherited both the good and the bad.
These were the giants of old,
Men of renown.
In those days, only strength was admired.
Winning in battle amid violent slaughter—
This was called the ultimate virtue.
To achieve glory this way gave them their titles—
Conquerors,
Gods,
Sons of gods.
Their true name should have been Destroyers and Plagues.
This is the way people will achieve fame on Earth.
The things that are truly worthy of fame will be hidden.

The man you saw is your seventh great-grandson.
He was the only righteous man in a perverse world.
Therefore, he was hated for daring to be good.
He told them the truth—
That God would come to judge them.
God wrapped him in a cloud
And carried him away in a heavenly chariot
Pulled by winged horses.
He walks with God above
He didn't have to die.
This is the reward of the good.
Now see the punishment that awaits the rest.

Narrator:

Adam looked and saw that things had changed.
The war had stopped,
And now everything was fun and games.
They were feasting,
Dancing,
Indulging themselves.
Some married and some used prostitutes.
They committed rape and adultery
Whenever a beauty caught their eye.
Drunkenness and fighting followed.

Finally, an older man rose up.
He told them what they were doing was wrong.
He went to their gatherings
And preached to them about conversion and repentance.
But it didn't do any good.

The elder stopped fighting and moved far from them.
On a mountain he began to build a huge boat.
It was covered with pitch,
With a large door in the side.
He set aside provisions for men and beasts.
Then something strange happened.
The animals came by twos and by sevens—
Beasts,
Birds,
Insects.
They entered the boat.
Last came the old man and his three sons and their wives.
The wind rose from the south.
Dark clouds gathered,
Full of all the mists and vapors of the sky,
Until like a dark ceiling, they covered the skies.
The rain rushed down, a torrent to cover the Earth.
The boat was lifted up and rode, tilting over the waves.
Every building was washed away,

And along with their cities, all their arrogance drowned.
Sea covered sea.
There were no shores.
Sea monsters swam in luxurious palaces.
The only people left were those in the boat.

Adam grieved to see his descendants die.
A flood of tears and sorrow drowned his face.
He fell to his knees.
Then the angel raised him up.
He wasn't able to comfort Adam.
Who could be comforted when all his children are lost?

Adam:

I wish I had never seen this vision!
It would have been better to be ignorant.
Then I would have only my own sin and punishment to bear.
Each day has enough evil of its own.
The sorrows of all the ages have come on me at once.
Because of me, all these things shall happen.
It torments me to know that this must happen.
Let no man desire to look into the future.
No one should be told what will happen to himself or his children.
He can be sure his future holds evil.
When he sees it, he will grieve ahead of time.
It's better to wait and grieve when it actually happens.

The people on the boat
Floating on a watery desert
Will eventually die from grief and hunger.
I had hoped when war on Earth ended,
That things would have gone well.
I hoped peace would be the result.
But I see now that peace can corrupt people
Just like war does.
Why is it like this?
Tell me, does mankind end there on that boat?

Michael:

You saw the winners of the war,
How they had much strength
And no virtue.
They spilled much blood
And created much destruction.
They were famous, exalted, and rich.
But those things changed their course
From death and gore in war,
To pleasure, laziness, gluttony, and lust.
In the middle of peace, they choose war.

Those who lost the war
Also lost virtue
And the fear of God.
They had no help from God in the battle
Because their religion was fake.
And afterward, they even forgot to pretend.
From the end of the war going forward
All they could do was live the best they could,
For good or for evil,
On the meager lands their conquerors left them.
All shall turn to sin.
All are depraved.
They forgot justice.
They forgot temperance.
They forgot truth and faith.
There was only one man left,
The only light in that dark age.
He was a good example.
He didn't fear violence or mocking.
He admonished them for their behavior.
He told them how to be good,
How to follow the paths of righteousness.
He warned them of God's wrath.

God told the man to build a wonderous ark.
You saw that, Adam.
He could then save himself and his household
From a world that had turned to destruction.
As soon as the man and his family and all the animals
Got on board the ark,
The Heavens opened,
Pouring rain down day and night.
All the fountains of the deep woke,
Filling the oceans until they flooded the land.
Even the highest hills were covered.
Eden itself was moved out of its place.
The lush greenery was destroyed.
The trees floated down to the open sea.
They settled on a bare, salty island,
Where only seals and whales go.
This will teach you that no place is sacred.
The only places that can be holy
Are places where the men who live there are holy.

But now look what will happen next.

Narrator:

Adam saw the ark floating on the receding waters.
The clouds were gone,
And a north wind blew gently on the waters.
The Sun shone bright on the glassy sea.
The deep stopped pouring forth water.
The waters ran softly toward the deep.
Then the ark was no longer floating,
But rested firm on a high mountain.
Rocks appeared, and the waters flowed toward the sea.

A raven flew out from the ark.
After the raven, a dove was released.
The dove was sent to look for green trees and solid ground.

The second time the dove came back, it had an olive leaf—
A sign of peace.
Soon, dry ground appeared.
The old man came out of the ark.
His family followed him.
He lifted his hands to the Heavens
And praised God for his deliverance.
Over his head was a rainbow, full of color.
This spoke of peace with God
And a new covenant.

At this, Adam's heart rejoiced.

Adam:

Oh, Teller of Future Things!
How this makes my heart glad
To see that mankind—
And all the creatures—
Shall live and not die!
My sadness is far less now,
Even though I saw so much destruction.
For one man was so perfect and righteous
That God promised to raise another world from him.
But what does the ribbon of color in the sky mean?
Is it a sign of God's acceptance?
Is it holding back the waters in the clouds?

Michael:

You can see clearly how God is willing to forgive.
Even though the whole Earth was full of violence
And all mankind was corrupt,
God, finding one good man, relented.
He did not blot out mankind.
God made a covenant never to destroy the Earth by flood again,
Nor to make the seas flow over the lands,
Nor to let the rains drown the world,

Killing all men and beasts.
From now on, when the storms rise,
The three-colored rainbow will be in the clouds,
Reminding mankind of God's covenant.
Day and night,
Seed time and harvest,
Heat of summer and frosty winter—
These shall stop.
Fire will consume all the old,
And the world will be remade,
Heaven and Earth,
As a home for the righteous.

BOOK 12 REFERENCES

Canna *(place):* Canaan (Canna) was the land in which Abraham would settle.

Egypt *(place):* A country in north Africa; In the Bible, Egypt was both a source of oppression, as in the case of the enslavement of the Israelites, and refuge, as when Mary and Joseph fled to Egypt to protect the baby Jesus from Herod's murderous intentions.

Hermon *(place):* The northern border of the promised land in the Bible

Jordan River *(place):* The boundary of the promised land, the Jordan River is also an analogy for the crossing between life and death.

Mount Carmel *(place):* Site of Elijah's defeat of the prophets of Baal in the Bible (I Kings 18)

Shechem *(place):* Shechem was the first portion of the promised land given to Abraham and was also the location of the Israelites covenant with God under Joshua.

Ur of Chaldea *(place):* In the Bible, Ur of Chaldea was the home of the patriarch, Abraham. It was part of the Sumerian civilization and was in the region of today's Iraq.

BOOK 12

Michael finishes the story of sin and explains God's plan of salvation. Then he escorts Adam and Eve out of Paradise.

Narrator:

Just as a traveler stops to rest at noon,
Here the Archangel Michael paused.
He had completed the tale of the world destroyed.
He had yet to tell of the world restored.

Michael:

You have seen the world begin and end.
You have seen mankind reborn from a second father.
There is still much you have not seen of the destruction.
But I see you are tired.
Thinking of divine things will exhaust mortals.
So I will go ahead and tell you what is coming.

They were the only ones left,
This second father of mankind and his close family.
The judgment of the flood was fresh in their minds.
They lived in fear of God.
They thought about right and wrong.
Many children were born to them.
They worked the soil and grew crops—
Corn
Wine
Oil.
They took bulls, lambs, and goats
And sacrificed them to God with wine and feasting.
There was joy and peace for many years.

Eventually one arose who was proud and ambitious.
He was not content with equality and brotherhood.
He rose up and ruled his brothers,
He didn't respect harmony and law.
He hunted—and it was men, not beasts, who were his prey.
He killed or captured those who didn't submit to him.
He was called a Mighty Hunter,
But his name means "rebel."
With others like him, he marched west from Eden,
And found black lava boiling from the ground like vomit.
This is the very mouth of Hell.
From the waste products of Hell,
He built a city and a tower,
Tall enough to reach to Heaven.
This tower was built so it could be seen from far away,
So that no one would forget him.
God, who walks among men unseen,
Came there before the tower was high enough to reach Heaven.
Angrily, He sent a quarrelsome spirit on them.
This spirit drove out their native languages.
Their voices became a jangling noise of unknown words.
A hideous clamor rose from the mob of builders.
They called to each other until they were hoarse,
But no one understood.
Heaven laughed to see the confusion.
The building was abandoned,
And the works of their hands were named "Confusion."

Adam:

What a terrible son this was,
To want power over his brothers.
God did not give one man power over another.
God told us to rule the beasts and fish and birds alone.
Only God Himself may be the ruler of men.
With regard to each other, each man is free.
But this rebel didn't just want to be greater than his brothers.
He wanted to be greater than God.

Wretched man!
What does he think he's going to eat up there in the clouds?
He won't have either bread to eat or air to breathe up there!

Michael:

You're right to detest that grandson of yours.
For he will bring much trouble on men,
As he tries to overthrow rational liberty.
But on the other hand,
True liberty has already been lost,
Just as correct reason has been.
For rational thought and liberty always go together.
As soon as reason is clouded or ignored,
Immediately the passions overrule the mind.
Man becomes a slave to these passions,
Even though before he lost his reason, he was free.
If any man permits passions to rule instead of reason,
God will enslave him to cruel leaders.
They will take away his outward freedom as well.
Tyranny is inevitable—
Even though this is no excuse for anyone to become a tyrant.
Some nations will fall far from virtue—
Which is reason.
Because of this, justice will take away their outward freedom
Just as they gave away their inward freedom.
Look at the son of the man who built the ark—
He shamed his father,
And all his descendants were cursed to a lifetime of slavery.
Mankind will go from bad to worse,
Until God, tired of their sin,
Will turn his face away,
And leave them to their filthy ways.

God will select one nation from all that exist.
One faithful man will rise up from that nation.
He will be raised to worship idols.
Can you believe that men would be so stupid

As to turn their backs on the living God,
And worship wood and stone?
This man will bring his family into a land God will show him.
From him, God will raise a mighty nation.
God will give him His blessing.
In his seed, all nations will be blessed.
The man will obey God,
Even though he doesn't know where God is taking him.
He will leave his gods,
His friends,
His land, Ur of Chaldea,
And with his servants and herds and flocks,
Will trust all his riches to the God who called him.
He will settle in Canna.
I see his tents pitched around Shechem.
There, God promised to give the land to his descendants.
From Hermon to the western sea,
On the shore of Mount Carmel,
By the river Jordan.
Ponder this—
All the nations of the Earth
Shall be blessed by his seed.
That seed will be your great deliverer.
He shall bruise the serpent's head.
You will see this more clearly soon.
This patriarch was blessed,
And was given the name Abraham.

He will leave a son and a grandson,
Who are wise and faithful like he is.
The grandson will have twelve sons.
He will go to a land called Egypt on the river Nile.
Can you see it, splitting into seven mouths as it reaches the sea?
In time of famine, he will go to Egypt,
Invited there by his younger son.
The younger son's good deeds
Will lead him to be second in command,
Just beneath Pharaoh.

There this man will die,
And leave his people to grow into a nation.

Many years later, another king will rise.
He will try to stop the growth of this nation.
Instead of guests in the land,
He will make them slaves.
He will kill their baby boys.
This will go on until two brothers sent by God
Named Moses and Aaron
Will lead them back to their promised land.

But first, the tyrant who denies God
Must be forced by signs and judgments to let them go.
The signs will be severe—
From a river turned to blood,
To frogs, lice, and flies,
From rotting, dying cattle
To rashes all over his skin—
And over all his people—
From thunder mixed with hail,
And hail mixed with fire,
Devouring the crops—
And what the fire doesn't devour,
The locusts will.
Nothing green will be left on the ground.
Darkness so thick you can feel it
Will blot out three days.
Last of all, at the stroke of midnight,
All the first born of Egypt will die.
After these ten wounds,
The River Dragon will be tamed.
He will let the travelers leave.
He will humble his heart,
But not for long.
Just like ice is harder after a thaw,
So will Pharaoh's heart be.
He will chase after the people he set free.

God will be with them as an angel,
Going before them in a cloud by day,
And in a pillar of fire at night.
He will guide them on their journey.
The stubborn Pharaoh will pursue them,
But God will give Moses power.
When he raises his staff,
The sea will swallow Pharaoh and his army,
But it will let God's people pass on dry land.
God will give Moses power to do this.
The chosen nation will move through the desert toward Canaan.
Going through the desert is not the easiest way
But it will keep them safe from war.
If war scares them,
They might flee back to Egypt in fear,
Choosing a low life of servitude.

They will spend their years in the desert
Forming a government and a senate,
And receiving God's law from Mount Sinai.
Some of the laws will be about civil justice.
Some will be for religious rites of sacrifice.
This sacrifice will tell the nation,
By types and shadows,
About the seed who will bruise the serpent's head,
And how He shall do it.
Because God's voice is dreadful to the human ear,
They will have Moses listen to God for them,
And tell them what God said.
By this we know that no man can approach God
Without a mediator.
Moses is the mediator at that time,
But a greater one will come.

After the giving of the law,
God will delight in obedient men.
He will set up His tabernacle among them.
The Holy One will dwell there.

God will give them instructions
How to build a sanctuary of cedar and gold.
The ark of the covenant will be in it,
And in the ark will be the records of the covenant.
Over that will be a mercy seat of gold,
Between the wings of two cherubim.
Before God seven lamps will burn,
Representing the heavenly fires.
A cloud will rest over the tent by day,
And a fiery gleam by night.
Finally, they will come to the land promised to Abraham
And to his seed.

The rest of the story is too long to tell.
Many battles will be fought.
Many kings will be destroyed.
Many kingdoms will be won.
And the Sun will stand still in Heaven
Until Israel claims Canaan.

Adam:

On you who are sent from Heaven!
Enlightener of my darkness!
You have told me great things,
Especially about Abraham and his seed.
For the first time, my eyes are opening,
And my heart begins to relax.
I was worried about what would become of me
And all mankind.
Now I see the day is coming
When all the nations will be blessed.

I don't deserve this goodness.
I reached for forbidden knowledge.
I disobeyed God.
But there's one part I don't understand.
Why did God give them so many laws?

They must have been quite sinful to need so many laws.
How can God reside with people like these?

Michael:

Don't doubt it—
Sin will rule them.
They're your offspring, after all.
The law was given to stir up their sin to fight.
When they see the law,
They can see their sin.
They can't erase their sin.
They can try with their weak, piddling efforts.
They can sacrifice bulls and goats.
But they'll see that animal blood is not enough.
Someone just must pay for the unjust.
In *that* righteousness, they can be given faith.
In *that* righteousness, they can find justification before God.
In *that* righteousness, they can find peace of conscience.
They can't find those things in the law.
They can't find those things in ceremonies.
They can't find those things by trying to be good.

The law appears imperfect.
It can't fix their problems
But its purpose is to point them to a better covenant.
They will be led from types to truth,
From flesh to spirit,
From law to grace,
From fear to sonship,
From works to faith.
Even though God loved Moses,
And he was the minister of the law,
It was Joshua whose name was given to the savior—
Called Jesus by the Gentiles.
It is he who will overcome the serpent
And bring man back to Paradise.

In the meantime,
Israel will live and prosper in Canaan.
When their sins interrupt their peace,
God will raise up enemies
To bring them to repentance.
First they will be saved through judges,
And later through kings.
The kings, known for their reverence and good deeds,
Will receive a promise—
That their throne will endure forever.
Out of David the King,
A Son will arise.
This One will be the seed of the woman,
The One I told you about.
This is the One Abraham trusted.
He will be the last King.
His reign will never end.

But first, a long line of kings must rule.
The son of David will come first.
He will be known for wealth and wisdom.
Until that king, David's son,
The ark of the covenant will live in a tent.
But this king will build him a glorious temple.

The kings who will come next will be both good and bad.
But more of them will be bad.
Their foul idolatry and other sins
Will make God so angry
That he will give their land,
Their city,
His temple,
His holy ark,
And all that was in it
To Babylon.
He will let his people languish in captivity.
After seventy years He will bring them back.
He will remember His covenant with David

And His mercy toward them.
First they will rebuild,
And for a while they will live modestly.
But once they grow rich in wealth and in population,
They will begin to fight.
But the fights will begin among the priests.
The ones who tend the altar should be the most peaceful.
Their fighting will pollute the temple.
At last, they will seize the scepter.
They will have no thought that David's descendants should rule.
Finally, the kingship will pass into the hands of strangers.
And because of this,
The time will be right for the Messiah to be born.

At His birth, a new Star will proclaim that He has come.
It will guide wise men from the East.
They will ask where He is,
So they can offer incense, myrrh, and gold.
An angel will tell the shepherds the place of His birth.
They will hurry there gladly,
And the song of the angels will be heard overhead.
A virgin will be His mother.
He will be fathered by the power of the Most High.
He will become the King
Who sits on the hereditary throne of David.
He will reign on Earth,
But his glory will rise up to the Heavens.

Narrator:

Michael stopped talking here.
He saw that Adam was drowning in tears of joy.

Adam:

Oh prophet of glad tidings!
Now I understand what I was looking for.
I understand why our hope is in the Seed of the woman.

Hail the Virgin Mother,
Even though she shall be my descendant,
From her womb shall the Son of God come.
Because of this, God will unite with mankind.
The serpent should be watchful now—
His fatal bruise is coming with heavy pain.
Tell me when and where they will fight.
Tell me what blow will strike the Savior's heel!

Michael:

Don't think of their fight as a duel.
Don't think about a literal head
Or a literal heel.
That's not how the Son will join mankind to God.
It's not by His strength that he shall overcome.
Satan gave you death.
The Savior will bring you the cure.
He won't do this by destroying Satan.
He will do it by destroying Satan's works in you.
He will do it by fulfilling the call to obedience to God.
He will suffer death,
Taking your penalty for you,
And for your descendants.

This is the only way justice can be done.
God's law will be fulfilled,
First by His life of obedience,
But more so by His love.
For love is the fulfillment of the law.
He will take your punishment
By coming in the flesh.
He will live a perfect life,
And die a cursed death.
He will bring life to all who believe in His redemption.
His obedience will be given to those who believe.
His good deeds will be counted as theirs.

Because of this, He will be hated.
He will be blasphemed.
He will be seized forcefully.
He will be judged and condemned to death.
He will die a shameful death,
A cursed death,
Nailed to the cross.
He will be killed by His own countrymen,
Slain for bringing life.

And on the cross, His enemies will be nailed.
The law will be crucified with Him.
The sins of all mankind will be crucified with Him.
Sin can never again hurt those who trust in Him.
He will die.
But he will soon come back to life.
Death has no power over Him.
Before the third sunrise,
The morning Stars will see Him rise.
Your ransom will be paid.

He will redeem all who embrace Him by faith—
A faith that is accompanied by good works.
This godly act nullifies your doom.
This is the death you should have died because of your sin.
This death will bruise Satan's head,
Crush his strength,
And defeat Sin and Death,
Which are the two main arms of Satan.
Sin and Death will attack Satan
Far more deeply than they will bruise the Victor's heel,
Far more deeply than they will bruise those who are His.
A believer's death will be like sleep,
Gently floating into eternal life.

He will not stay long on Earth after the resurrection.
He will stay only long enough to appear
To His disciples, those who still follow Him in this life.

He will commission them to teach all the nations of Him.
They will teach about salvation
They will baptize those who believe,
For baptism is the sign of guilt being washed away.
Baptism washes them from sin to life.
They will be pure in mind,
And ready to die like their Savior did.
They will teach all nations,
For from the day of the resurrection,
Not only the Jews will be saved,
But all the nations.

Then the Savior will ascend to Heaven,
Victoriously soaring through the air,
Triumphing over his enemies—and yours.
He will surprise the serpent,
The prince of the air,
And chain him
And drag him away.

He will take his seat at God's right hand.
When it is time for the world to end,
He will come with glory and power
To judge the living and the dead.
He will judge the unfaithful dead,
But He will reward the faithful,
And receive them into happiness,
Whether in Heaven or Earth.
For then, Earth shall be all Paradise.
It will be even happier than Eden was.

Adam:

Oh, what infinite goodness!
Evil shall be turned to good!
This is more wonderful than creation was before all this happened.
Light out of darkness!
I don't know whether to repent of my sin,

Or just rejoice over and over again.
To God be all glory.
Grace will triumph over wrath.

But if the Savior is going up to Heaven,
What will happen to the few who are faithful?
Won't they be left alone in the middle of their enemies?
Who will guide them?
Who will defend them?
Won't the unfaithful ones be crueler to the faithful
Than they were to Him?

Michael:

You can be sure of that.
But He will send a Comforter down from Heaven.
His Spirit will live in them.
The Spirit will write the law of faith on their hearts.
He will guide them in all truth.
He will give them spiritual armor
So they can stand against Satan's attacks,
And put out his fiery arrows.
What can men do to them?
They won't be afraid,
Even if they have to die.
They will have consolation from the Spirit.
They will be so peaceful,
Their enemies will be amazed.

The Spirit will be poured out on the Apostles first.
Then on all those who are baptized.
They will receive wonderful gifts,
Speaking in tongues,
Working miracles,
Just like their Savior did before them.
They will win great numbers of all nations
To receive the good news from Heaven.

Once their ministry is done,
Their race well run,
And their story written,
They will die.

Then wolves shall infiltrate the church.
They will use the good news
For their own ambitions,
For their greed,
For money.
They will taint the truth with superstitions and traditions.
Only the Bible will stay pure.
The wolves will give themselves names and titles,
Trying to become powerful.
They will pretend to be spiritual.
They will pretend to have the Spirit of God.
They will use the power of the government
To force people to follow spiritual laws,
The laws that can only be engraved on the heart by the Spirit.
They will take away liberty.
They will tear down believers.
Persecution will arise against all who worship in spirit and in truth.
The rest will think that religious ceremonies are enough.
Truth will fade away.
Works of faith will be rare.
The world will go on like this,
Cruel to good men,
Decent to bad men.

But the day will come when the good will be refreshed,
And vengeance will come on the wicked.
The Savior will return,
Coming on the clouds from Heaven,
Displayed in the glory of the Father.
He will dissolve Satan,
And his perverted world.
He will raise a new Heaven and a new Earth
Out of the burning pyre of what went before.

They will be established with righteousness,
And peace,
And love,
Bringing forth joy and bliss.

Adam:

You have told the whole story.
Beyond this is the abyss.
Beyond this is eternity,
Which no one can see the end of.
I will go from here quite educated.
I will go from here with great peace.
I am full of knowledge.
I have no room for any more.
From hereon I know:
It is best to obey.
It is best to love and fear God,
To walk like He is right next to me,
To depend on Him,
To understand His mercy,
To overcome evil with good.
Small, weak things will overcome strong, worldly-wise things
Suffering for the sake of truth is the highest victory.
For the faithful, death is the gate to life.
I have been taught by His example.
My Redeemer is ever blessed.

Michael:

Now that you know this, you have all wisdom you need.
Don't hope for more.
If you knew every Star by name,
And all the powers of the air,
And all the secrets of the deep,
And all the workings of nature,
And all the works of God,
And even if you had all the riches of the Earth,

And all the power to rule,
The only thing you still need is good deeds.
Add faith,
Virtue,
Patience,
Temperance,
Love, which is called charity,
And is the heart of all the others.
With these, you won't be sorry to leave Paradise.
You will have a paradise inside you.

Let's go down from this high hill of speculation.
It is time for us to part.
The guards camping on the hill over there are waiting for me.
We can't stay any longer.
Go wake up Eve.
I have sent her gentle dreams.
She is ready to be submissive and meek.
When you think she is ready,
Tell her the things you have learned,
Mainly how by her Seed,
All mankind will be delivered.
Live together in faith,
Sorry for the evil you have done,
But cheered by meditating on the happy end of the story.

Narrator:

Michael finished speaking, and they both went down from the hill.
Adam went to where Eve was.
She was awake.

Eve:

I know where you went.
And I know where you came from.
God is in my sleep,
And He gave me dreams.

I fell asleep full of sorrow,
But he sent me dreams of great good.
I will go where you lead.
You're everything to me.
Because of me, you lost this Paradise.
Even though all is lost because of me,
By me, through the promised Seed,
All shall be restored.

Narrator:

Adam was pleased with her words,
But he didn't say anything.
The Archangel was nearby.

The cherubim were bright on the hill.
They descended and floated like a mist, going home.
They held the sword of God before them,
Bright as a comet.
It scorched the land.

The Angel caught Adam and Eve by the hand.
He led them to the eastern gate,
And down the cliff to the plain.
Then he disappeared.
When they looked back, all was ablaze.
They wept
But then wiped their tears.
They had the whole world before them.
They had providence for their guide.

And hand in hand,
With wandering, slow steps,
They went on their way alone.

THE END

REFERENCE INDEX

Acheron *(Book 2; place):* The river of pain in the underworld of ancient Greek mythology

Achilles *(Book 9.1; man):* Hero of Homer's *Iliad*, dies in the Trojan War

Adonis *(Book 1; god):* In ancient Greek mythology, Adonis is the epitome of masculine beauty and the lover of several goddesses, especially Aphrodite

Aeneas *(Book 9.1; man):* Hero of Virgil's *Aeneid*, founds a new settlement for the displaced Trojans after the Trojan War

aether *(Book 3; reference):* According to ancient and medieval cosmology, as well as pre-19th century scientists, aether was the fifth element, after earth, fire, air, and water. The aether was the substance through which light waves traveled and was present in space outside of the Earth's atmosphere. There is still uncertainty about the existence of aether.

alchemist *(Book 5; person):* Medieval scientist concerned with turning other metals into gold

Amphisbaena *(Book 10.2; animal):* Mythical snake with a head at both ends.

Argus *(Book 11.1; giant):* In ancient Greek mythology, Argus is a giant with a hundred eyes who served as a watchman.

Athens *(Book 9.2; place):* Athens was the heart of ancient Greece, the place where democracy was founded.

Baalam *(Book 1; man):* Biblical prophet who refused to curse Israel (see Numbers 22-24); Also known for encouraging the Israelites to defile themselves with Midianite women (Numbers 31:16)

Babel *(Book 3; place):* In the Bible, Babel is the site of a tower built to reach to the heavens. God confused the languages of those building it, so they weren't able to complete the tower.

Camelot *(Book 1; place):* The mythical British kingdom of King Arthur

Canna *(Book 12; place):* Canaan was the land in which Abraham would settle.

Cerastes *(Book 10.2; animal):* Mythical horned snake that hides itself in the sand with only its horns protruding in order to lure prey.

Charlemagne *(Book 1; man):* King of the Franks and Lombards; Later the first Holy Roman Emperor (lived 747-814 AD)

cherub (cherubim is plural) *(Book 1; angel):* Winged angelic beings who guarded the Tree of Life after the fall of man; See Ezekiel 10:9-17 for a description

Cocytus *(Book 2; place):* The river of wailing in the underworld of ancient Greek mythology

Cusco *(Book 11.1; place):* The capital of the Inca Empire in Peru and still a major city in that country. Also spelled Cuzco.

Delilah *(Book 9.2; woman):* In the Bible, Delilah was Samson's lover. She betrayed him to the Philistines, bringing about his downfall.

Dipsas *(Book 10.2; animal):* Mythical snake whose bite would cause extreme thirst

Eden *(Book 4; place):* The original home of Adam and Eve in the Bible, a garden of paradise

Egypt *(Book 12; place):* A country in north Africa; In the Bible, Egypt was both a source of oppression, as in the case of the enslavement of the Israelites, and refuge, as when Mary and Joseph fled to Egypt to protect the baby Jesus from Herod's murderous intentions.

Elisha *(Book 11.1; man):* Elisha was a Biblical Old Testament prophet who served under the prophet Elijah, and saw his mentor carried off to Heaven in a chariot of fire.

Ellops *(Book 10.2; animal):* Mythical sea serpent; also can be spelled Elops

Elysian fields *(Book 3; place):* Part of the ancient Greek underworld, the Elysian fields were akin to paradise, where the good and brave souls went after death.

Empedocles *(Book 3; man):* Philosopher who theorized that all matter was made of four elements: earth, water, air, and fire

Furies *(Book 10.2; goddesses):* Ancient Greek goddesses of vengeance

Hera *(Book 9.1; goddess):* Wife of Zeus and queen of the Greek gods, known for her jealousy

Hermon *(Book 12; place):* The northern border of the promised land in the Bible

Homer *(Book 9.1; man):* Ancient Greek who wrote the Iliad and the Odyssey

Hydrus *(Book 10.2; character):* Mythical creature that, when eaten by a crocodile, would eat its way out, killing the crocodile. Most often depicted as a kind of water snake, but also believed by some to be an otter, an eel, or a bird.

Isis *(Book 1; goddess):* Egyptian goddess later worshipped by the ancient Greeks and Romans

Israel *(Book 1; people):* The people of God in the Old Testament of the Bible

Jacob *(Book 11.1; character):* In the Bible, Jacob, later named Israel, was the patriarch of the twelve tribes of Israel. In a dream he had a vision of a ladder reaching to heaven, with angels going up and down. In the dream, God promised him many descendants through whom all the earth would be blessed.

Jordan River *(Book 12; place):* The boundary of the promised land, the Jordan River is also an analogy for the crossing between life and death.

King Charles *(Book Intro; character):* John Milton was a strong supporter of the Parliamentarian side in the English Civil War—the side that favored disposing of kings. King Charles I believed that it was God's will that he should be king, and his son after him. When his reign began to list toward abuse of power, King Charles I was executed, and for eleven years, England had no king. In 1660, Charles II was placed upon the throne, reinstituting the English monarchy.

Lavinia *(Book 9.1; woman):* In Virgil's *Aeneid*, Lavinia is the princess Aeneas marries.

Lethe *(Book 2; place):* The river of forgetfulness in the underworld of Ancient Greek mythology

Leviathan *(Book 1; animal):* Enormous sea beast spoken of in Job 41 and Psalm 74:14, often identified as a sea serpent, dragon, or (later) a crocodile or whale

Limbo *(Book 3; place):* In Roman Catholic doctrine, Limbo is the border between Heaven and Hell, a holding place for the dead prior to the resurrection of Christ and their salvation and for unbaptized believers.

Maeonides *(Book 3; man):* Homer, author of the *Iliad* and the *Odyssey*

Mary *(Book 5; woman):* The virgin Mary, mother of Jesus

Medusa *(Book 2; woman):* In Greek mythology, Medusa is a woman who was cursed to have living snakes as hair. A single glance at her hideousness was enough to turn a person to stone.

Mercury *(Book 5; god):* Roman messenger god who had winged sandals and hat

Moloch *(Book 1; reference):* Canaanite god who was known for enjoying child sacrifices

Montezuma *(Book 11.1; man):* Emperor of the Aztec Empire in the early 1500s, Montezuma was killed during the Spanish conquest of Mexico.

Mount Carmel *(Book 12; place):* Site of Elijah's defeat of the prophets of Baal in the Bible (I Kings 18)

Mount Niphates *(Book 3; place):* The place Satan lands on Earth

Mount Olympus *(Book 7; place):* In Greek mythology, Mount Olympus is the home of the gods.

Mount Zion *(Book 3; place):* While Mount Zion can refer to a particular hill in Jerusalem, it's also a symbol of God's kingdom, the hill from which He rules.

Muse(s) *(Book 1; goddess):* Greek goddesses of the arts, said to inspire poetry, music, and stories

Osiris *(Book 1; god):* Egyptian god of death and rebirth

Phineas *(Book 3; man):* Blind king from ancient Greek mythology who was also a seer

Phlegethon *(Book 2; place):* The river of fire in the underworld of ancient Greek mythology

phoenix *(Book 5; animal):* Mythological bird that is said to die and come to life again

Rome *(Book 9.2; place):* Rome was the capital of the ancient Roman Empire.

Samson *(Book 9.2; man):* In the Bible, Samson is a judge (leader) of Israel. He was known for his superhuman strength and for his weakness for woman.

seraph *(Book 5; angel): A* variety of Biblical angel with six wings. In the Bible, Samson is a judge (leader) of Israel. He was known for his superhuman strength and for his weakness for woman.See Isaiah 6.

Shechem *(Book 12; place):* Shechem was the first portion of the promised land given to Abraham, and was also the location of the Israelites covenant with God under Joshua.

Solomon *(Book 9.2; man):* In the Bible, Solomon is the son of King David, and ruled after him, building a lavish temple for God.

Styx *(Book 2; place):* The river of hate in the underworld of the ancient Greeks.

the Sultan *(Book 11.1; man):* Byzantium, the remnant of ancient Rome, was conquered by the Ottoman Empire in 1453 A.D. and was thenceforward (until 1922 A.D.) ruled by a sultan.

Thamyris *(Book 3; man):* Ancient Greek singer condemned to blindness after he challenged the Muses to a musical contest and lost

Tigris River *(Book 9.1; place):* The book describes the Tigris River as springing forth from Eden, going underground, and coming up as a fountain by the Tree of Life. Historically, the Tigris River is one of the boundaries of Mesopotamia (the other being the Euphrates River). It flows through the current countries of Turkey, Iraq, and Syria.

Tiresias *(Book 3; man):* Blind prophet from ancient Greek literature

Troy *(Book 1; place):* Site of the Trojan War, the subject of Homer's *Iliad*

Turnus *(Book 9.1; man):* In Virgil's *Aeneid*, Turnus was betrothed to Lavinia, but she is destined to marry Aeneas.

Ur of Chaldea *(Book 12; place):* In the Bible, Ur of Chaldea was the home of the patriarch, Abraham. It was part of the Sumerian civilization and was in the region of today's Iraq.

Urania *(Book 7; goddess):* The Greek muse of the Heavens, who can inspire deep philosophical thought

Venus *(Book 1; goddess):* Roman goddess of love and sexuality

Zion *(Book 3; place):* The holy land of God, sometimes referring to a specific hill in Jerusalem, sometimes to Jerusalem itself, and sometimes to a more spiritual land of God

BIBLIOGRAPHY

"John Milton." *Encyclopædia Britannica*, Encyclopædia Britannica, inc., 25 Oct. 2024, www.britannica.com/biography/John-Milton.

Lewis, C. S. *A Preface to Paradise Lost*. Oxford University Press, 1961.

Milton, John. *Areopagitica and Of Education With Autobiographical Passages from Other Prose Works*, Edited by George H. Sabine. Appleton-Century-Crofts, 1951

Milton, John. *Paradise Lost: A Poem in Twelve Books, A New Edition*. The Odyssey Press, Bobbs-Merrill Educational Publishing, 1977.

SneakerBlossom.com

SneakerBlossom
Books

www.ingramcontent.com/pod-product-compliance
Lightning Source LLC
Chambersburg PA
CBHW070917120626
46546CB00001B/297